ADVERSE POSSESSION IN PROPERTY MATTER – SUPREME COURT'S LATEST LEADING CASE LAWS

CASE NOTES- FACTS- FINDINGS OF APEX COURT JUDGES & CITATIONS

JAYPRAKASH BANSILAL SOMANI

Dedicated

To

All the Past & Present Judges of the Supreme Court of India.

Salute to their wisdom.

Salute to their interpretation of Law.

Salute to their elaborative judgement writing.

SUPREME COURT OF INDIA

Contents

Contents

Preface

Dear Learned Advocates of the Civil Courts, High Courts, Supreme Court, Individuals, Officers etc,

I am very delighted to provide you a book on 'ADVERSE POSSESSION IN PROPERTY MATTER - SUPREME COURT'S LATEST LEADING CASE LAW'

In this book you will get...

1. Name of the Case i. e. Cause title

2. Relevant Sections discussed in the case

3. Hon'ble Judges/Coram of the case

4. Number of PDF Pages in Original Judgement of the case

5. All available Citations of the case

6. Case Note with appeal allowed/ dismissed or disposed off

7. Facts of the case

8. Hon'ble Apex Court's findings, while dismissing/allowing or disposing the appeal

9. Ratio Decidendi if any.

My special thanks to Manupatra, because of their web portal I can compile this book in well manner. I am also thankful to Notion Press to support me to publish & market this book throughout the Country. Thanks to my Juniors, Advocate Colleagues & Insolvency Professional Colleagues to support me in this venture.

Adv. Manoj Kumar Chowdhary & Miss. Pooja Arvind Rai has helped me a lot to compile this book. I hope this book will add some value addition in the wealth of your legal knowledge. Your positive feedbacks will boost me to compile/ write further books & negative feedbacks will improve my skills. Kindly send your valuable feedbacks by email.

Thanks with Regards,

Jayprakash B. Somani

Advocate, Supreme Court of India

Email: jaysomani64@gmail.com

Web Site: www.jayprakashsomani.com

Call: 9322188701, 8459194576

Acknowledgements

Printed & Published by
Notion Press
No. 8, 3rd Cross Street,
CIT Colony, Mylapore,
Chennai, Tamil Nadu- 600004
Managed by
Jayprakash Somani Advocates & Solicitors
Law Firm for Supreme Court of India
Delhi Office
B- 851, 1st Floor, Shivaji Marg, New Ashok Nagar, Delhi 110096.
Call: 9322188701, 8459194576
Supreme Court Chamber
312, 3rd Floor, M. C. Setalvad Block, In front of 'D' Gate, Bhagwan Das
Road, Supreme Court of India, New Delhi 110001
Contact: 8459194576, 9811011747
www.jayprakashsomani.com

Books are available online in India
1.Notion Press:https://notionpress.com/author/jayprakash_somani
2.Amazon:https://www.amazon.in/s?k=jayprakash+somani
3.Flipkart:https://www.flipkart.com/search?q=Jayprakash%20Somani
Books are available online at International Market
4. Amazon International: https://www.amazon.com/
s?k=jayprakash+somani
5. Amazon United Kingdom: https://www.amazon.co.uk/
s?k=jayprakash+somani
6. E-Books/Kindle edition at National & International Level:
https://www.amazon.in/s?k=jaypraksh+somani

Sabir Ali Khan vs. Syed Mohd. Ahmad Ali Khan and Ors. (13.04.2023 - SC) : MANU/SC/0377/2023

Relative Section:

WAQF ACT, 1995 - Section 52; Section 112;

LIMITATION ACT, 1963 - Section 27

Hon'bleJudges/Coram:

K.M. Joseph and Hrishikesh Roy

Equivalent Citation: 2023(3)ALD29, 2023(2)CTC856

NumberofPagesintheOriginalJudgment: 34

Case Reference:

M. Ismail Frauqui and Ors. v. Union of India (UOI) and Ors. MANU/SC/0860/1994;

Mosque known as Masjid Shahid Ganj and Ors. v. Shiromani Gurdwara Parbandhak Committee and Anr. MANU/PR/0024/1940;

Mohammad Shah v. Fasihuddin Ansari and Ors. MANU/SC/0114/1956;

Moattar Raza and Ors. v. Jt. Director of Consolidation, U.P. Camp at Bareilly and Ors. MANU/UP /0075/ 1970;

Khilli Ram v. State of Rajasthan MANU/SC/0394/1984;

Chhedi Lal Misra (Dead) through Lrs. v. Civil Judge, Lucknow and Ors. MANU/SC/7104/2007;

Wali Mohammed (Dead) by Lrs. v. Rahmat Bee and Ors. MANU/SC/0131/1999;

Fazlul Rabbi Pradhan v. State of West Bengal MANU/SC/0345/1965;

Syed Yousuf Yarkhan and Ors. v. Syed Mohammed Yarkhan and Ors. MANU/SC/0294/1967;

M. Siddiq (D) thr. L.Rs. v. Mahant Suresh Das and Ors. MANU/SC/1538/2019;

Karnataka Board of Wakf v. Government of India and Ors. MANU/SC/0377/2004;

Mohd. Ismail v. Sabir Ali MANU/SC/0391/1962; Ahmed G.H. Ariff and Ors. v. Commissioner of Wealth Tax, Calcutta MANU/SC/0167/1969;

T. Kaliamurthi and Ors. v. Five Gori Thaikal Wakf and Ors. MANU/SC/3330/2008;

Chintamani Sahoo and Ors. v. Commissioner of Orissa Hindu Religious Endowments and Ors. MANU/OR /0063 /1983;

Gulam Ali Saha and Ors. v. Sultan Khan and Ors. MANU/OR/0027/1967;

Srinivasa Reddiar and Ors. v. N. Ramaswamy Reddiar and Ors. MANU/SC/0350/1965;

Chinna Jeeyangar Mutt, Thirupathi v. C.V. Purushotham and Ors. MANU/AP/0115/1974;

The State Wakf Board, Madras v. Subramanyam and Ors. MANU/TN/0285/1977;

Syed Mohiuddin Ahmed and Ors. v. Sofia Khatun and Ors. MANU/WB/0076/1940;

U.P. Sunni Central Board of Waqif and Anr. v. Smt. Hasan Jehan Begum and Anr. MANU/UP/0006/1977;

Anisur Rahman and Ors. v. Sheikh Abul Hayat MANU/BH/0113/1965;

Hemanta Kumari Bose v. Iswar Sridhar Jiu and Ors. MANU/WB/0150/1946;

Govinda Jiew Thakur and Ors. v. Surendra Jena and Ors. MANU/OR/0044/1961;

V. Rajaram v. Ramanujam Iyengar and Ors. MANU/TN/0083/1963;

Central Board of Secondary Education and Ors. v. Aditya Bandopadhyay and Ors. MANU/SC/0932/2011;

C. Beepathumma and Ors. v. V.S. Kadambolithaya and Ors. MANU/SC/0209/1963;

(Smt.) Amina Khatoon v. Third Addl. D.J. Farukhabad and Ors. MANU/UP/0915/1987 : 1987 All LJ 1282;

K.S. Viswam Iyer (Dead) Through Lrs. v. State Wakf Board, Madras 1994 Suppl. (2) SCC 109;

Naba Kishore Panda v. Bulendra MANU/OR/0219/1974 : (1974-40 Cut LT 1152;

Arjuna Jena v. Chaitanya Thakur MANU/OR/0104/1978 : (1978) 45 Cut LT 461;

Shri Chiranjilal Patwari v. Commr., Hindu Religious Endowments, Orissa, Bhubaneswar MANU/ OR/0271 / 1973 : (1974) 40 Cut LT 41;

Sambari Bewa v. Orissa Board of Wakfs Second Appeal No. 361 of 1966;

Abdul Fatah Mohammad Ishak v. Russomy Dhar Chaoudhary 22 Indian Appeals 76

Case Note:

Civil - Adverse possession - Beneficiary of wakf - Sections 52and 52(1) of Waqf Act, 1995, Sections2(2)(i), 38 and 38(1) of U.P. Muslim Waqfs Act, 1936 and Sec 27and 107 of Limitation Act, 1963- Controller of Waqf Board invoked Section 52(1) of Act and directed Collector to recover and deliver possession of disputed land from unauthorised occupants-Respondents - It was thereupon that Collector directed Respondents to deliver possession of property to Waqf Board within thirty days-Respondent filed Appeal before Waqf Tribunal which stand allowed and order of Collector was set aside -Revisions was filed against said order by Appellants before High Court - High Court had affirmed order passed by Tribunal on ground that first Respondent had perfected title by adverse possession - Hence, present appeal - Whether beneficiary of waqf could succeed on strength of plea of adverse possession in regard to property of waqf and High Court was correct in finding that action was barred as it was not Article 96 of Limitation Act, which applied but Article 65 of Limitation Act, 1963.

Facts:

The Controller of the Waqf Board passed Order. By the said Order, he invoked Section 52(1) of the Act and directed the Collector to recover and deliver possession of the disputed land from the unauthorised occupants. It was thereupon that the Collector passed Order directing the Respondents to deliver possession of the property to the Board within thirty days. This Order came to be challenged by the first Respondents in the Appeals, viz., the alleged unauthorised occupants before the Additional District Judge. The said Appeals were allowed by the Additional District Judge. The Appellant filed Writ Petition contending that it was the Waqf Tribunal which had the jurisdiction and not the Additional District Judge. This contention found favour with the High Court and it was found that the Additional District Judge did not possess jurisdiction. The Order of the

Additional District Judge came to be set aside. Thereafter, the first Respondent filed Appeal before the Waqf Tribunal. The Waqf Tribunal allowed the Appeals and the Order of the Collector was set aside. It was the said Order, which has been confirmed by the High Court by passing the impugned Order, by which, the Revision Petitions filed by the Appellant, came to be dismissed. The High Court had affirmed the Order passed by the Tribunal, however, on the ground that the first Respondent, in the Appeals, had perfected title by adverse possession.

Held, while dismissing the appeal:

(i) As far as the first sale was concerned, the sale was not effected by the Mutawalli or the Manager of the Waqf. The sale was effected by the brother of the Mutawalli. Therefore, the High Court was correct in finding that Article 96 would not come to the aid of the Appellant. [20]

(ii) The 1936 Act applied to Wakfs created before or after the commencement of the Act. However, Section 2(2) declares that the Act shall not apply to certain waqfs. They included a waqf whereunder not less than seventy five per cent of the total income, after deduction of certain sums, was for the time being payable for the benefit of the waqif or his descendants. However, Section 38(1) of the 1936 Act made it clear that every waqf, whether subject to the Act or not and whether created or after the commencement of the 1936 Act, shall be registered. Proceeding on the basis that the waqf was waqf-alal-aulad and which, in terms of Section 2(2)(i), was not subject to the provisions of the 1936 Act, it was compulsorily registrable in view of Section 38(1). Any waqf which was registered under the 1936 Act would also be deemed to be registered under the 1960 Act. That is, though the 1936 Act did not apply to certain wakfs, but when it comes to registration under Section 38, it was mandatory for every wakf to be registered whether subject to the Act and whether created before the Act or not. Thus, the registration of the Wakf was in fact compulsory under Section 38 of the 1936 Act. [50]

(iii) The argument that Section 107 of the Act would assist the Appellant in tiding over the bar of limitation did not appeal to this court. Section 107 of the Act, no doubt, proclaims that nothing in the Limitation Act, 1963 shall apply to any suit for possession of the immovable property comprised in any waqf or for possession of any interest in such property. [69]

(iv) A contention was taken that the Court was not dealing with a suit and the matter arises from a proceeding under Section 52 of the Act. It was contended that in regard to Section 52 the bar of limitation for a suit was inapplicable. This court had noticed that the debate in the High Court essentially centered around the question whether Article 96 would apply and applying the same, the Appellant could get around the impact of Article 65 read with Section 27 of the Act. This court had found that Article 96 had no application. Even in regard to a proceeding under the Act be it Section 52 if as on the date the action was taken, the title in the property stood vested with the person in possession by virtue of Section 27 of the Limitation Act then it may not be permissible to ignore the right which had been acquired. The decision in T. Kaliamurthi would apply in the facts and the action was barred. [72]

CHAPTER TWO

B.R. Patil vs. Tulsa Y. Sawkar and Ors. (09.02.2022 - SC) : MANU/SC/0182/2022

Relative Section:

Code of Civil Procedure, 1908 (CPC) - Order I Rule 3,

Code of Civil Procedure, 1908 (CPC) - Order II Rule 2,

Code of Civil Procedure, 1908 (CPC) - Order II Rule 3;

Constitution of India - Article 136,

Constitution of India - Article 142;

Hindu Succession Act, 1956 - Section 8;

Karnataka Court-fees And Suits Valuation Act, 1958 - Section 35(1)

Hon'bleJudges/Coram:

K.M. Joseph and Hrishikesh Roy, JJ.

Equivalent Citation: 2022(2)ALD266, 2022(3)BLJ209, 2022 (2) CCC 109 , 2022(3)CivilCC(S.C.), 2022(3)HLR57, 2022(3)ICC877, 2022/INSC/165, 2022(2)J.L.J.R.89, 2022(2)PLJR51, 2022(2)RCR(Civil)178

Case Reference:

Iswar Bhai C. Patel v. Harihar Behera and Ors. MANU/SC/0173/1999;

P. Lakshmi Reddy v. L. Lakshmi Reddy MANU/SC/0083/1956;

Secretary of State for India in Council v. Debendra Lal Khan MANU/PR/0072/1933;

Govindrao and Anr. v. Rajabai and Anr. MANU/PR/0076/1930;

Md. Mohammad Ali (Dead) by Lrs. v. Jagadish Kalita and Ors. MANU/SC/0785/2003;

Vidya Devi (Dead by L.R's) v. Prem Prakash and Ors. MANU/SC/0345/1995;

Mohd. Zainulabudeen (since Deceased) by Lrs. v. Sayed Ahmed Mohideen and Ors. MANU/SC/0322/1989;

Darshan Singh and Ors. v. Gujjar Singh (Dead) by Lrs. and Ors. MANU/SC/0007/2002;

Radhamoni Debi v. Collector of Khulna MANU/PR/0007/1900 : 27 Ind App 136;

Corea v. Appuhamy LEX/SLCA/0084/1910 : 1912 AC 230;

N. Varada Pillai v. Jeevarathnammal MANU/PR/0125/1919 : AIR 1919 PC 44;

Culley v. Deod Taylerson (1840) 3 P & D 539 : 52 RR 566

NumberofPagesintheOriginalJudgment: 15

Case Note:

Civil - Suit for Partition - Rejection sought - Non-joinder of necessary parties - All properties also contended to be not scheduled for the purpose of partition - Part decree directed by Trial Court - High Court allowed the appeal by Respondents herein - Hence the present appeal - Whether the suit originally filed was liable to be dismissed on the grounds raised by Appellant herein?

Facts:

Appellant was impleaded as first Defendant in the suit. The said suit was filed by his sister as the first Plaintiff and his sister-in-law as the second Plaintiff seeking partition and separate possession of their $1/5^{th}$ share each, in the suit Schedule items. The Trial Court partly decreed the suit. It granted prohibitory injunction in favour of the second Plaintiff. Three appeals were preferred. By the impugned judgment, the High Court has allowed the appeal filed by the Plaintiffs and the second Defendant and dismissed the appeal filed by the first Defendant. Hence the present appeal.

Held, while dismissing the Appeal:

The Code of Civil Procedure indeed permits a Plaintiff to join causes of action but it does not compel a Plaintiff to do so. The consequences of not joining all claims arising from a cause of action may be fatal to a Plaintiff. However, that would at any rate not advance the case of the Appellant. Hence for all these reasons, we are of the view that contention of the Appellant, must fail.[17]

In the facts of this case, on the cause of action which is projected in the plaint and the Schedule of properties which has been made by the Plaintiffs, the non-joinder of the uncle of the Appellant or his legal representatives would imperil the suit filed by the Plaintiffs.[18]

The very essence of adverse possession and therefore ouster lies in a party setting up a hostile title in himself. The possession of a co-owner is ordinarily on his behalf and also on behalf of the entire body of the co-owners. In the case of an ouster, the co-owner must indeed have the hostile animus. He must assert a title which is not referable to lawful title. Though the learned Counsel for the Appellant points out that this possession started prior to 1977 in that the Appellant was residing with his father in item No. 3 house from somewhere in the early seventies and he continued to reside after his father's death in the year 1977, when Shri R.M. Patil died in the year 1977, his possession in 1977, was clearly referable to lawful title as a co-owner entitled to inherit Under Section 8 of the Hindu Succession Act, 1956.Obviously, he cannot be permitted to set up adverse possession or ouster in the year 1977. [27]

Trial Court has also framed an additional issue No. 2, on 'partial ouster' as it were and answered the issue against the Appellant. Therefore, this is a case where the Appellant has against him concurrent findings of two Courts and in this appeal which is generated by special leave. [28]

The appeals are only maintained against the preliminary decree by which shares have been declared. Therefore, no reason to go into the question about the allotment of properties which is a matter to be gone into in the final decree proceedings. As to what is to be actual division of the properties, it is for the Appellant to raise such contentions as are available in this regard.[30]

Therefore, no merit in the appeals and thus dismissed. [31]

Mohinder Singh (Dead) through L.Rs. and Ors. vs. Narain Singh and Ors. (14.03.2023 - SC) : MANU/SC/0237/2023

Relative Section:

DELHI MUNICIPAL CORPORATION ACT, 1957 - Section 507;
DELHI MUNICIPAL CORPORATION ACT, 1957 - Section 2,
DELHI MUNICIPAL CORPORATION ACT, 1957 - Section 12

Hon'bleJudges/Coram:

Ajay Rastogi, C.T. Ravikumar and Bela M. Trivedi

Equivalent Citation: AIR2023SC1427, 2023/INSC/223

Case Reference:

Om Prakash Agarwal and Ors. v. Batara Behera and Ors. MANU/SC/0148/1999;

Umed Singh v. Government of National Capital Territory of Delhi and Ors. MANU/DE/0970/1997;

Smt. Indu Khorana v. Gram Sabha and Ors. MANU/DE/0969/2010

NumberofPagesintheOriginalJudgment: 13

Case Note:

Civil -Urbanization of area - Application of Act - Sections 33 and 64 of Delhi Land Reforms Act, 1954 and Sections 507(a), 507(b) and 507(c) of Delhi Municipal Corporation Act, 1957- Respondents had purchased from

Bhumidhar by registered sale deed and they applied for mutation under Act, 1954 and their names were mutated - Appellants later challenged mutation order opened in favour of Respondents claiming adverse possession by filing appeal under Section 64 of Act 1954 -Financial Commissioner set aside order of mutation passed in favour of Respondents holding that transfer was in contravention of Section 33 of Act, 1954 and further ordered land in dispute to be vested in Gaon Sabha - Respondents challenged said order by filing Writ Petitionbefore Single Judge of High Court which stand dismissed - Further, Division Bench of High Court returned finding that once notification had been published in exercise of power under Section 507(a) of Act, 1957 which expressly urbanizes subject land in question, it no more remains rural area thus, all proceedings under the Act, 1954 stand non est leaving parties to agitate their claims before appropriate fora - Hence, present appeal - Whether Division Bench erred in holding that once rural area was urbanized by issuance of a notification under Section 507(a) of Act, it ceases to be governed by provisions of Delhi Land Reforms Act, 1954.

Facts:

The Respondents had purchased land from Bhumidhar by a registered sale deed. Later, they applied for mutation under Act, 1954 and their names were mutated.It had been pleaded by the Appellants that before the registered sale deed came to be executed by bhumidharin favour of the Respondents and their names were mutated, the Appellants had come into possession over the subject land. The Appellants later challenged the mutation order opened in favour of the Respondents claiming adverse possession by filing appeal under Section 64 of the Act 1954. After certain rounds of litigation, the Financial Commissioner set aside the order of mutation passed in favour of the Respondents holding that the transfer was in contravention of Section 33 of the Act, 1954 and further ordered the land in dispute to be vested in Gaon Sabha. The Respondents challenged the Orderby filing Writ Petition before the Single Judge of the High Court which came to be dismissed. In further appeal, the Division Bench of the High Court returned a finding that once the notification had been published in exercise of power under Section 507(a) of the Act, 1957 which expressly urbanizes the subject land in question and brings within the scope and ambit of Act, 1957, it no more remains rural area thus, all proceedings under the Act, 1954 standnonest leaving the parties to agitate their claims/ disputes before appropriate fora.

Held, while dismissing the appeal:

(i) Once there is a notification issued by the competent authority in exercise of power under Section 507(a) which is a special provision in reference to rural areas, such of the rural areas cease to be included therein upon issuance of the notification and shall thereafter include in and form part of the urban areas in terms of the notification. Sub-clause (b) and (c) of Section 507 deals with the nature of grant of exemption or levy of taxes for such of the areas falling within the scope and ambit of the Act, 1957. [31]

(ii) Once a notification has been published in exercise of power under Section 507(a) of the Act, 1957, the provisions of the Act, 1954 cease to apply. In sequel thereto, the proceedings pending under the Act, 1954 become non est and loses its legal significance. [36]

(iii) What persuaded this Court was that even after upholding the judgment of the Division Bench of the High Court, it gives a fresh life to the Respondents to go ahead in taking possession of the subject property despite the fact that registered sale deed was executed in their favour by Bhumidhar but they were still deprived of possession and the defence of the Appellants in counter was that they were in possession of the subject land by adverse possession. At the same time, this Court may also record that the registered sale deed executed in favour of the Respondents by Bhumidharwas never the subject matter of challenge and no such proceedings were pending in the Court of law. [42]

(iv) In the given facts and circumstances, in exercise ofpower and to do complete justice to the parties, this court direct the Appellants to hand over physical possession of the subject land free from all encumbrances to the Respondents within a period of two months from the date of passing of this Order. If the Appellants fail to hand over possession within the time stipulated, it would be open to the Respondents to make an application to the concerned jurisdictional Judicial Magistrate and after obtaining necessary orders with assistance of the local administration may proceed for taking possession of the subject land. [44]

Disposition:

Appeal Dismissed

State of Maharashtra vs. Pravin Jethalal Kamdar (Dead) by Lrs. (07.03.2000 - SC) : MANU/SC/0157/2000

Relative Section:

Constitution Of India - Article 226,

Constitution Of India - Article 32;

Indian Contract Act, 1872 - Section 72;

Urban Land (ceiling And Regulation) Act, 1976 [repealed] - Section 27,

Urban Land (ceiling And Regulation) Act, 1976 [repealed] - Section 27(1),

Urban Land (ceiling And Regulation) Act, 1976 [repealed] - Section 6(1)

Hon'bleJudges/Coram:

Saiyed Saghir Ahmad and Y.K. Sabharwal

Equivalent Citation: AIR2000SC1099, 2000(2)BLJ838, 2001(103(1))BOMLR460, 2000 (1) CCC 314 , JT2000(3)SC29, 2000(2)SCALE239, (2000)3SCC460, [2000]2SCR134, 2000(2)UJ836

Case Reference:

Maharao Sahib Shri Bhim Singhji v. Union of India and Ors. MANU/SC/0509/1980; Mafatlal Industries Ltd. v. Union of India MANU/SC/1203/1997;

Ajudh Raj and Ors. v. Mofi s/o Mussadi MANU/SC/0369/1991

NumberofPagesintheOriginalJudgment: 4

Case Note:

Limitation - possession - Articles 58 and 65 of Limitation Act, 1963 - possession had been taken pursuant to void documents - Article 65 applied under which period of limitation for suit for possession of immovable property based on title is 12 years from date of adverse possession - suit not barred by limitation.

Facts:

1. The respondent, now represented through his legal heirs, is the original plaintiff in a suit for declaration and possession filed against the appellant State of Maharashtra and others. The suit was filed on 22nd August, 1976, seeking a declaration that the order dated 26th May, 1976 by which the right of pre-emption was exercised by defendants 1 and 2 (State of Maharashtra and Deputy Collector and Competent Authority Urban Land Ceiling, Nagpur respectively) to purchase the property in question and the sale deed dated 23rd August, 1976, obtained from the plaintiff in pursuance of the said order was null and void and do not confer any right title or interest in the property in favour of defendants. A decree for possession was also sought against refund of Rs. 2.60.000/- received by the plaintiff under the sale deed dated 23rd August. 1976. The facts in brief and in respect whereof, there is hardly any dispute are:

2. The Urban Land (Ceiling and Regulation) Act, 1976 (for short, 'the Act') came into force for the State of Maharashtra w.e.f. 17th February, 1976. The plaintiff claims that he was not holding any land in excess of the ceiling limit prescribed under the Act and, therefore, was under no obligation to file a return under Section 6(1) of the Act before the competent authority, The plaintiff wanted to sell the suit property to his relations and business acquaintances with whom he entered into an, agreement of sale dated 31st March, 1976 for sale of the suit property for consideration of Rs. 2,60,0007-. Section 27(1) of the Act required the plaintiff and the prospective purchaser to obtain permission from the competent authority under the Act to sell the suit property. According to the plaintiff, the application for grant of the said permission to sell the property to prospective purchaser was rejected by the competent authority by order dated 26th May, 1976 and further by the same order, the competent authority exercised option to buy the property on behalf of the State of Maharashtra. The plaintiff was offered the same consideration which was to be paid to the plaintiff by the prospective purchaser, i.e., Rs, 2.60.000/-. Thus, pursuant to the order dated 26th May, 1976, passed under Section 27 of the Act, a sale deed dated 23rd August, 1976 was executed between the plaintiff and the State

of Maharashtra and possession was also taken over by defendant No. 3, namely. Deputy Commissioner of Sales Tax, Eastern Division, Nagpur. Since then, the suit property is in possession of defendant No. 3.

3. In Maharao Sahib Shri Bhim Singhji v. Union of India MANU/SC/ 0509/1980 : AIR1981SC234 this Court upheld the validity of the Act except Section 27(1) insofar as the said provision imposed a restriction on transfer of any urban or urbanisable land with a building or a part of such building, which was within the ceiling limit. Section 27(1) to the extent it sought to affect the right of a person to dispose of his urban property within the ceiling limit was held invalid. In view of this decision, the plaintiff claimed in the suit that the order dated 26th May, 1976 and sale deed executed pursuant thereto on 23rd August, 1976 were null and void since what was sought to be sold to the prospective purchaser was the properly within the ceiling limit and the plaintiff was entitled to a decree of declaration that the impugned order and the sale deed are illegal and invalid and do not confer right of ownership on defendants. The possession taken pursuant to above was claimed to be illegal and thus the plaintiff is entitled to recovery of possession besides damages for wrongful use and occupation at the average market rental value of the property. It has also been pleaded that the plaintiff was ready and willing to return the amount of Rs. 2,60.000/- paid to him under the sale deed dated 23rd August, 1976.

4. The suit was dismissed by the trial Court. In the appeal reversing the decision of the trial Court, the High Court has passed a decree for possession in favour of the plaintiff on his deposit of sum of Rs. 2,60.000/- which has been directed to be paid to the defendants/appellants. Under these circumstances, the State of Maharashtra has filed the present appeal.

Held by Hon'ble Supreme Court:

1. Article 58 of the Limitation Act, 1963. prescribes limitation of three years from the date when the right, to sue first accrues to obtain a declaration. Under Article 65, the period of limitation prescribed for filing a suit for possession of immovable property or any interest therein based on title is 12 years from the date when possession of the defendants becomes adverse to the plaintiff. The contention urged on behalf of the State Government was that Article 58 of the Limitation Act was applicable as the plaintiff had sought declaration about the invalidity of the order dated 26th May, 1976 and sale deed dated 23rd August, 1976 and that the period of limitation of three years had to be computed from 26th May, 1976 and, therefore, the suit filed on 22nd August, 1988 was hopelessly barred by

time. This contention was rejected by the High Court as also by the trial Court. The contention urged on behalf of the plain tiff and which has been accepted is that the suit is basically for possession of the property based upon title and the sale deed dated 23rd August, 1976 and the order dated 26th May, 1976 being void ab initio and without jurisdiction, a plea about its invalidity can be raised in any proceedings and it is not necessary to claim any declaration and thus Article 65 which deals with suit for possession based on title would be applicable from the date, the possession of the defendant becomes adverse to the plaintiff. The High Court held that in view of the order and the sale deed being null and void and without jurisdiction, the same have no existence in the eyes of law and the plea about invalidity of these documents can be raised in any proceedings and no separate declaration is necessary to be sought. It held that the suit for possession would be governed by Article 65 of the Limitation Act, 1963. It was further held that a suit is within time even from the date when the possession of the suit property was taken on the execution of the sale deed on 23rd August, 1976.

2. As already noticed, in Bhim Singhji's case, MANU/SC/0509/1980 : AIR1981SC234 (supra) Section 27(1) insofar as it imposes a restriction on transfer of any urban or urban sable laid with a building or a portion of such building, which is within the ceiling area, has been held to be invalid. Thus, it has not been and cannot be disputed that the order dated 26th May, 1976, was without jurisdiction and nullity. Consequently, sale deed executed pursuant to the said order would also be a nullity. It was not necessary to seek a declaration about the invalidity of the said order and the sale deed. The fact of plaintiff having sought such a declaration is of no consequence. When possession has been taken by the appellants pursuant to void documents, Article 65 of the Limitation Act will apply and the limitation to file the suit would be 12 years. When these documents are null and void, ignoring them a suit for possession simpliciter could be filed and in the course of the suit it could be contended that these documents are nullity. In Ajudh Raj v. Mofi S/o Mussadi MANU/SC/0369/ 1991 : [1991]2SCR690 this Court said that if the order has been passed without jurisdiction, the same can be ignored as nullity, that, is, non-existent in the eyes of law and is not necessary to set it aside; and such a suit will be governed by Article 65 of the Limitation Act. The contention that the suit was time barred has no merit. The suit has been rightly held to have been filed within the period prescribed by the Limitation Act.

3. Next, it was contended that simply on account of Section 27(1) to the extent stated above having been declared unconstitutional, it does not follow that the petitioner is entitled to equitable relief particularly when he accepted the sale consideration and executed the sale deed. Reliance has been placed on the decision of Mafatlal Industries Ltd. v. Union of India MANU/SC/1203/1997 : 1997(89)ELT247(SC) holding that equitable considerations cannot be held to be irrelevant in case of claim for refund under Section 72 of the Contract Act or in a writ petition filed under Article 226 or 32 of the Constitution. That was a case where refund was not directed despite invalidity of the provisions under which duties had been paid or collected as person claiming the refund had passed on the burden of duty to others and had not suffered any prejudice or loss and, therefore, no directions were issued for refund. It was held that under these circumstances there is no question of reimbursement to such a person. The principles laid down in Mafatlal Industries case have no applicability to the facts of the present case. It cannot be said that the plaintiff has not suffered any prejudice or loss. It is not a case of a voluntary sale. The plaintiff had to execute the sale deed on account of an illegal and without jurisdiction order made under Section 27(1) of the Act in respect of property within the ceiling limit. If the plaintiff has retained the sum of Rs. 2,60,000/- all these years, at the same time, defendants have also retained the possession of the property. The plaintiff on his own did not want to sell the property to the defendants/appellants. The fact that the same amount of consideration as mentioned in the agreement of sale was paid to the plaintiff by the defendants, is of no relevance. On the facts of the case, it cannot be held that there are any equitable considerations against the plaintiff to warrant the denial of relief of possession granted to him by the High Court.

4. For the foregoing reasons, the appeal is dismissed leaving the parties to bear their own costs.

The Principal Secretary, Revenue Department, State of Telangana and Ors. vs. B. Rangaswamy (dead) by L.Rs. and Ors. (11.07.2022 - SC) : MANU/SC/0830

Relative Section:

Andhra Pradesh Land Encroachment Act, 1905 - Section 14;

Andhra Pradesh Survey And Boundaries Act, 1923 - Section 14;

Code of Civil Procedure, 1908 (CPC) - Order XLI Rule 27;

Code of Civil Procedure, 1908 (CPC) - Section 80;

Constitution of India - Article 142;

Limitation Act, 1963 - Schedule - Article 58

Hon'bleJudges/Coram:

Indira Banerjee and A.S. Bopanna

Equivalent Citation: 2022(5)ALD9, 2022/INSC/686

Case Reference:

The Management of State Bank of Hyderabad v. Vasudev Anant Bhide and Ors. MANU/SC/0326/1969;

Town Municipal, Council, Athani v. The Presiding Officer, Labour Courts, Hubli and Ors. MANU/ SC/0331 /1969;

Banarsi Das v. Kanshi Ram and Ors. MANU/SC/0302/1962;

Daya Singh and Ors. v. Gurdev Singh (Dead) by L.Rs. and Ors. MANU/
SC/0012/2010; Rukhmabai v. Laxminarayan and Ors. MANU/SC/0186/
1959;

Ramanbhai Ashabhai Patel v. Dabhi Ajitkumar Fulsinji and Ors. MANU/
SC/0319/1964;

Jamshed Hormusji Wadia v. Board of Trustees, Port of Mumbai and Ors.
MANU/SC/0033/2004;

Chikkam Koreswara Rao v. Chikkam SubbaRao and Ors. MANU/SC/
0347/1970; Nagubai Ammal and Ors. v. B. Shama Rao and Ors. MANU/SC/
0089/1956;

Sita Ram Bhau Patil v. Ramchandra Nago Patil (Dead) by Lrs. and Ors.
MANU/SC/0285/1977;

ADIL Jamshed Frenchman (D) by Lrs. v. Sardar Dastur Schools Trust
and Ors. MANU/SC/0108/2005;

Wadi v. Amilal and Ors. MANU/SC/0729/2002;

Network Inc. v. K.R. Mohan Reddy MANU/AP/0944/2006;

H.S. Goutham and Ors. v. Rama Murthy and Ors. MANU/SC/0073/
2021;

Shivajirao Nilangekar Patil v. Mahesh Madhav Gosavi MANU/SC/0120/
1986 : (1987) 1 SCC 221

NumberofPagesintheOriginalJudgment:17

Case Note:

Property - Ownership - High Court held that, there was land belonging
to the government wedged between the property bearing Survey No. 129/
73 and Survey No. 129/56, Hence present appeal -Whether the Plaintiffs
proved their title to the suit Schedule property?

Facts:

Issue in present case is with regard to ownership of suit property. The
trial court on analysing the evidence has arrived at its conclusion that
Plaintiffs failed to prove that the suit Schedule property admeasuring 2 acres
10 guntas is part and parcel of Survey No. 129/56. In that view, since the
identity and correctness of the suit Schedule property was not proved, the
said issues were held against the Plaintiffs in addition to the other findings
and the suit was dismissed. The High Court while considering the appeal,
though had reappreciated the evidence, has essentially found fault with the
Defendants in not producing the original of the documents which were
produced and marked. In that light, drawing an adverse inference against
the Defendants, arrived at a conclusion that the Trial Court had wrongly

held that there was land belonging to the government wedged between the property bearing Survey No. 129/73 and Survey No. 129/56. The High Court set aside the judgment of the trial court and decreed the suit. It is in that view, the Defendants claiming to be aggrieved are before this Court in this appeal.

Held, while allowing the appeal

1. It is evident that keeping in view the nature of the controversy, the oral evidence would not be sufficient to resolve the controversy relating to the identity of the property. Insofar as the Plaintiff No. 2 having entered into a sale transaction and having purchased an extent of 2 acres 10 guntas in Survey No. 129/56, the same cannot be in dispute since the same is under a registered document but the issue is; which was the property that was actually conveyed. Though for convenience a sketch was attached to the sale deed and it is marked as Exhibit A-4, in view of the dispute raised by the Defendants that there is a plot of government land to the east of Survey No. 129/73 being the west of Survey No. 129/56, this aspect of the matter requires consideration since the question essentially is as to whether the identity of the land is established by the Plaintiff with reference to the land which is purportedly purchased as land located in Survey No. 129/73 under another sale deed at Exhibit A-5. The sketch along with all the sale deeds are not an authenticated record but is prepared for the convenience inter se between the parties to the sale deed and does not bind anyone else. [21]

2. Further, though the Plaintiff No. 2 has got the sale deed in his favour as far back as in the year 1964, the documents to indicate the mutation proceedings and the revenue documents being mutated in favour of the Plaintiff has not been produced. The document at Exhibit A-10 and A-11 with regard to the notification relating to construction of Bhagyanagar Studios indicating the Schedule and the plan for construction of the studio cannot advance the case of the Plaintiff insofar as determining the real issue in the suit. The said notification indicates with regard to the construction in Survey No. 129/73 to the extent of 5 acres and the layout of the construction is shown only in Survey No. 129/73, over which the Defendants have no dispute whatsoever relating to that property, that too, when construction was well within the extent of 5 acres 38 guntas. The name of B. Rangaswamy (Plaintiff No. 2) indicated as neighbour's land to the said plan would not mean that the case of the Plaintiff had been accepted by the Defendants to be contiguous lands. All that was necessary at that stage for the relevant competent authority was to take note of the

permission sought for construction and grant approval to that extent. The dispute arose only when the compound wall beyond that extent was attempted to put up. [24]

3. A perusal of the judgment passed by the High Court would indicate that it has proceeded as if the burden which had been cast on the Defendant has not been discharged though the issues framed had cast the burden on the Plaintiff not only with regard to the title but also identity of the suit Schedule property and also correctness of the plaint Schedule property. It is noted that the High Court in fact has relied more on the oral evidence of the Plaintiff and has commented that the trial court has wrongly relied on the document at Exhibit B-1. The nature of the documents indicated above and the manner in which the Plaintiff was required to establish its case in a circumstance where it was claiming that the properties are contiguous was in the circumstance that there was a challenge raised by the Defendants to the identity and description of boundaries rather than title. It is in that context Exhibit B-3 that was addressed earlier in point of time and B-1 subsequently becomes relevant. As noted, the said documents were produced from the records of the Defendant and mere denial at this point of time more particularly when the dispute between the parties has continued ever since the Plaintiff purchased the property and sought to establish their right over the same. What is necessary to be taken note is that, excluding the property bearing Survey No. 403 with its old No. as 151/1 if the Plaintiff has purchased any other extent in Survey No. 129/56 the Defendants have no claim over the same. It is in that light, the High Court was required to examine the matter since what is to be established by the Plaintiff was the identification and correctness of the exact location of the land. [27]

4. The burden was heavier on the Plaintiff when the suit was instituted subsequently and in that context, the proof of the entire extent was necessary to be shown to prove the identity of the property which was purchased by the Plaintiff No. 2 and thus to establish the same not to be the property belonging to the government. [32]

5. In the instant case though the execution of a sale deed purportedly conveying an extent in Survey No. 129/56 was proved, the fact as to whether the extent as indicated in the sale deed was actually located in the Survey No. 129/56 was not established by the Plaintiffs. If that be the position, even if, the Plaintiffs had actually come in physical possession of the extent of property which is not actually situate in Survey No. 129/56 and is the property which is claimed as the government property, the

possession to be declared to have been perfected by adverse possession will have to pass the test to claim such right. It is in that context it was alternatively contended that the Plaintiffs had also stated that they have perfected their title by adverse possession. It is in that context that the Trial Court firstly having noted that there are no documents to indicate possession has also taken note that the purchase being in the year 1964 and the suit being filed in the year 1981 the statutory period of 30 years to acquire right by way of adverse possession also does not arise. The High Court no doubt has taken into account the evidence of PW-1 who has stated that he has been in possession from the date of purchase. The fact also remains that subsequently when the compound wall was constructed it was demolished and it is the very case of the Plaintiffs that since there was interference the suit was filed. Therefore, even if possession was taken by the Plaintiff, in the context of claiming title, there is no other material. Pursuant to the purchase, the mutation proceedings and the assessment for tax if any made has also not been brought on record by way of evidence. Therefore, in the context of the possession sought to be protected based on title, when the identity of the property is not established despite purchase claimed under the registered sale deed the relief as prayed for would not be available and therefore the Trial Court was justified in that regard. [34]

6. Judgment passed by the High Court is set aside. The judgment passed by the trial Court is restored. [36]

7. Appeals allowed. [37]

CHAPTER SIX

Baini Prasad (D) Thr. LRs. vs. Durga Devi (02.02.2023 - SC) : MANU/SC/0088/2023

Relative Section:

Constitution of India - Article 136;

Indian Evidence Act, 1872 - Section 115;

Transfer of Property Act, 1882 - Section 51

Hon'bleJudges/Coram:

B.R. Gavai and C.T. Ravikumar

Equivalent Citation: : AIR2023SC894, 2023(2)ALD214, 2023(2)ALT1, 2023(2)CivilCC(S.C.), 135(2023)CLT743, 2023/INSC/95, 2023(1)KLJ783, (2023)1MLJ809

Case Reference:

Janak Dulari Devi and Ors. v. Kapildeo Rai and Ors. MANU/SC/0553/2011;

Ram Prakash Sharma v. Babulal Birla and Ors. MANU/SC/0609/2011;

Ghisalal and Ors. v. Dhapubai (Dead) by L.Rs. and Ors. MANU/SC/0037/2011; Nedunuri Kameswaramma v. Sampati Subba Rao MANU/SC/0319/1962;

R.S. Madanappa and Ors. v. Chandramma and Ors. MANU/SC/0356/1965;

Pratima Chowdhury v. Kalpana Mukherjee and Ors. MANU/SC/0089/2014;

B.L. Sreedhar and Ors. v. K.M. Munireddy (Dead) and Ors. MANU/SC/1101/2002; The Chairman, State Bank of India and Ors. v. M.J. James MANU/SC/1069/2021; Abdul Kader Chaudhury v. Upendra Lal Barua and

Ors. MANU/WB/0265/1936;

Bodi Reddy v. Appu Goundan MANU/TN/0426/1970;

N.C. Subbayya v. Pattan Abdulla Khan (1956) 69 LW (Andhra) 52

NumberofPagesintheOriginalJudgment: 11

Case Note:

Property - Ownership - Section 51 of Transfer of Property Act, 1882 - Issue in present case is with regard to Suit for possession of land and challenge is to the order of High Court allowing the appeal of Respondent - Whether the reversal by the High Court of the modification effected by the First Appellate Court warrants interference in exercise of power under Article 136 of the Constitution of India.

Facts:

The Respondent herein (Plaintiff) filed Civil Suit for possession of land and for permanent prohibitory injunction restraining the Defendant (the Appellant h) from interfering on disputed land and other land appurtenant to it, owned by her. The suit was decreed and upon holding the Respondent herein/Plaintiff as the owner of the encroached land handing over the same after demolition of the structures put up there was ordered. The original Appellant/Defendant took up the matter in appeal. As per the judgment in Civil Appeal, the findings on ownership and the question of encroachment were confirmed. Nonetheless, the First Appellate Court modified the judgment and decree holding that the Plaintiff/Respondent herein is not entitled to recovery possession of 11 Biswancies of land after demolition of the structures put up thereon based on the principles of acquiescence. Consequently, she was found entitled to a decree of compensation at the market value prevalent at the time of filing of the suit in lieu of that relief and the compensation therefor was assessed at Rs. 5500. Over and above the said amount, the Respondent herein (the Plaintiff) was held entitled to recover interest at the rate of 12 % per annum from the date of filing of the suit till realization. RSA was filed challenging the modification of the judgment and decree of the Trial Court to above extent by the Respondent. As per the impugned judgment, the High Court allowed the Second Appeal and set aside the judgment and decree of the First Appellate Court for compensation to the Respondent in lieu of recovery of possession and the judgment and decree of the Trial Court for demolition and handing over of the possession of the encroached land was restored. The review petition filed by the Appellant in the said Second Appeal was dismissed by the High Court.According to the Appellants, the Respondent did not object and resort to civil remedy against the construction effected on the land in dispute within a reasonable time and, therefore, she is estopped from claiming recovery of the land in question after demolition of the structure raised thereon.

Held, while dismissing the appeal

1. A perusal of Section 51 of TP Act would reveal that even after the pre-requisites for the enforceability of equity enacted in it are satisfied, the right to election for one of the two alternatives provided under that Section would still rest with the person evicting. He may elect either to pay the value of improvements made by the Defendant who satisfies a description of "transferee" for the purpose of this Section and take the land or sell out his interests in the land to the transferee at the market value of the property, irrespective of the value of such improvements. [8]

2. Section 51 of TP Act is a general provision dealing with improvements effected by a transferee to the transferred property in the manner specifically provided thereunder. Thus, a bare perusal of Section 51, TP Act would reveal that in order to acquire the 'right to require' in the manner provided thereunder one should be a 'transferee' within the meaning of the TP Act and for the purpose of the said section. In short, Section 51 applies in terms to a transferee who makes improvements in good faith on a property believing himself to be its absolute owner. [9]

3. The original Appellant has failed to establish that he is a "transferee" within the meaning of the TP Act and for the purpose of Section 51, TP Act. In order to attract the Section the occupant of the land must have held possession under colour of title, his possession must not have been by mere possession of another but adverse to the title of the true owner and he must be under the bone fide belief that he has secured good title to the property in question and is the owner thereof. Section 51 gives only statutory recognition to the above three things. At the same time, in the case on hand, the concurrent findings of the courts below is that the Respondent herein is the owner of the land in question and the original Appellants had encroached upon it and effected construction. The Appellants herein have failed to establish the above mentioned three things. The evidence on record would also go to show that even the construction was effected in deviation of the approved plan. [10]

4. In the light of the concurrent findings on the questions of ownership and encroachment, it can only be held that it was after encroaching upon the land in question and ignoring the absence of any title that he made

structures thereon at his own risk. Once it is so found, the original Appellant cannot be treated as a 'transferee' within the meaning of the TP Act and for the purpose of Section 51, TP Act. Therefore, the Appellants are not entitled to rely on the provision Under Section 51, TP Act to seek for restoration of the modification made by the First Appellate Court with respect to demolition and possession. The Appellants, rightly, did not take up the plea of adverse possession and in the circumstances, being not a transferee for the purpose of Section 51 TP Act, he cannot legally require the Respondent either to pay the value of improvements and take back the land or to sell out the land to him at the market value of the property, irrespective of the value of the improvements. [11]

5. In the proven circumstances that the original Appellant was not having title over the property, that the Respondent herein is the owner of the land in question, that the concurrent finding is that the original Appellant was the encroacher and further that objection was raised by the Respondent herein against the construction she should not have shut out by the Rule of acquiescence or by the Rule of estoppel for having made a representation to make the original Appellant to believe that she had consented for the construction. [19]

6. The entire circumstances revealed from the evidence on record unerringly point to the fact that the Appellant had encroached upon land belonging to the Respondent and without bona fides effected constructions which is verandah which is extension of residential building. [20]

7. In a case where the owner of the land filed suit for recovery of possession of his land from the encroacher and once he establishes his title, merely because some structures are erected by the opposite party ignoring the objection, that too without any bona fide belief, denying the relief of recovery of possession would tantamount to allowing a trespasser/encroacher to purchase another man's property against that man's will. In Bodi Reddyv. Appu Goundan decision, the learned Judge held that in a suit for recovery of possession filed within the period of limitation provided under Limitation Act, the doctrine of laches or acquiescence has no place to defeat the right of the Plaintiff to obtain the relief on his establishing his title. In such a situation, in the absence of any misrepresentation by an act or omission, the mere fact after making objection the Plaintiff took some reasonable time to approach the Court for recovery of possession cannot, at any stretch of imagination, be a reason to deny him the relief him of recovery of possession of the encroached land on his establishing his title

over it. [21]

8. There is no flaw, legal error, perversity or patent illegality in the findings on the substantial questions of law by the High Court ultimately, in favour of the Respondent herein and in setting aside the judgment and decree of the First Appellate Court and also in restoring the judgment and decree of the Trial Court. [22]

9. Appeals dismissed. [23]

Ratio Decidendi:

Once owner of the land establishes his title, merely because some structures are erected by the opposite party ignoring the objection, denying the relief of recovery of possession would tantamount to allowing a trespasser to purchase another man's property against that man's will

Disposition:

Appeal Dismissed

A. Shanmugam vs. Ariya Kshatriya Rajakula Vamsathu Madalaya Nandhavana Paripalanai Sangam Represented by Its President and Ors. (27.04.2012 - SC)

Relative Section:

Code of Civil Procedure, 1908 (CPC) - Section 144;

Code of Civil Procedure, 1908 (CPC) - Section 30;

Constitution Of India - Article 142(1),

Constitution Of India - Article 226;

Specific Relief Act 1963 - Section 6

Hon'bleJudges/Coram:

Dalveer Bhandari and Dipak Misra

Equivalent Citation: 2012(114)AIC221, AIR2012SC2010, 2012(5)ALD41, 2012(3)ALLMR946, 2012(3)ALLMR(SC)946, 2012 (92) ALR 730, 2012(4)ALT5, 2012 (2) CCC 145 , 2012(3)RCR(Civil)1, 2012(4)SCALE666, (2012)6SCC430, [2012]4SCR74

Case Reference:

Alagi Alamelu Achi v. Ponniah Mudaliar MANU/TN/0279/1962 : AIR 1962 Mad 149;

Maria Margarida Sequeria Fernandes and Ors. v. Erasmo Jack de Sequeria (Dead) through L.Rs. MANU/SC/0225/2012 : (2012) 3 SCALE 550;

Dalip Singh v. State of U.P. and Ors. MANU/SC/1886/2009 : (2010) 2 SCC 114;

Mohanlal Shamji Soni v. Union of India MANU/SC/0318/1991 : 1991 Supp (1) SCC 271;

Ritesh Tewari and Anr. v. State of Uttar Pradesh and Ors. MANU/SC/ 0742/2010 : (2010) 10 SCC 677;

Jones v. National Coal Board [1957] 2 QB 55;

Chandra Shashi v. Anil Kumar Verma MANU/SC/0558/1995 : (1995) 1 SCC 421; James v. Giles et al. v. State of Maryland 386 U.S. 66 (1967) 87, S. Ct. 793;

United States v. J. Lee Havens 446 U.S. 620, 100 St.Ct.1912;

Ramrameshwari Devi v. Nirmala Devi MANU/SC/0714/2011 : (2011) 8 SCC 249; Enviro-Legal Action v. Union of India and Ors. MANU/SC/0837/ 2011 : (2011) 8 SCC 161;

Kavita Trehan v. Balsara Hygiene Products MANU/SC/0094/1995 : (1994) 5 SCC 380; Marshall Sons and Company (I) Ltd. v. Sahi Oretrans (P) Ltd. and Anr. MANU/SC/0079/1999 : (1999) 2 SCC 325;

Padmawati v. Harijan Sewak Sangh -CM (Main) No. 449 of 2002;

Ouseph Mathai and Ors. v. M. Abdul Khadir MANU/SC/0718/2001 : (2002) 1 SCC 319; South Eastern Coalfields Limited v. State of M.P. and Ors. MANU/SC/0807/2003 : (2003) 8 SCC 648; Zafar Khan v. Board of Revenue, U.P - MANU/SC/0251/1984 : (1984) Supp SCC 505;

Amarjeet Singh and Ors. v. Devi Ratan and Ors. MANU/SC/1843/2009 : (2010) 1 SCC 417;

Number of Pages in the Original Judgment: 22

Case Note:

Property - Legality of Order - Appeals arose out of cross suits filed before High Court - Single Judge of High Court set aside well-considered judgments of First Appellate Court - Hence, present Appeals - Whether any interference in impugned judgment was called for - Held, a well-reasoned judgment and a decree passed by trial Court ought not to have been reversed by First Appellate Court - Appellant had failed to prove adverse possession of suit property - Only by obtaining ration card and house tax receipts, Appellant could not strengthen his claim of adverse possession - High Court was fully justified in reversing judgment of First Appellate Court and restoring judgment of trial Court - Hence, no interference was called for - In case of Maria Margarida Sequeria Fernandes and Ors. v. Erasmo Jack de Sequeria (Dead) through L. Rs., this Court had laid stress on purity of pleadings in civil cases - Pleadings need to be critically examined by judicial officers or judges both before issuing ad interim injunction and/or framing of issues - Pleadings were foundation of litigation - It was bounden duty and obligation of parties to investigate and satisfy themselves as to correctness and authenticity of matter pleaded - Pleadings must set-forth sufficient factual details to extent that it reduced ability to put forward a false or exaggerated claim or defence - Pleadings must inspire confidence and credibility - Ensuring discovery and production of documents and a proper admission/denial was imperative for deciding civil cases in a proper perspective - In relevant cases, Courts should encourage interrogatories to be administered - Framing of issues was a very important stage of a civil trial - It was imperative for a judge to critically examine pleadings of parties before framing of issues - Unless wrongdoers were denied profit or undue benefit from frivolous litigations, it would be difficult to control frivolous and uncalled for litigations - Appellant was guilty of suppressing material facts and introducing false pleas and irrelevant documents - Appellant had also clouded entire case with pleas which had nothing to do with main controversy involved in case - All documents filed by Appellant along with plaint had no relevance to controversy involved in case - First Appellate Court had got into trap and was misled by documents and reached to an entirely erroneous finding that resulted in undue delay of disposal of a small case for almost 17 years - Appellant was guilty of introducing untenable pleas - Plea of adverse possession which had no foundation or basis in facts and circumstances of case was introduced to gain undue benefit - Court must be cautious in granting relief to a party guilty of deliberately introducing irrelevant and untenable pleas responsible for creating unnecessary confusion by introducing such documents and pleas - These factors must be taken into consideration while granting relief and/or imposing costs - It was bounden duty of Court to uphold truth and do justice - Every litigant was expected to state truth before law Court, whether it was pleadings, affidavits or evidence - Dishonest and unscrupulous litigants had no place in law Courts - Ultimate object of judicial proceedings was to discern truth and do justice - It was imperative that pleadings and all other presentations before Court should be truthful - Once Court discovered falsehood, concealment, distortion, obstruction or confusion in pleadings and documents, then Court should in addition to full restitution impose appropriate costs - Court must ensure that there was no incentive for wrong doer in temple of justice - Truth was foundation of justice and it had to be common endeavour of all to uphold truth and no one should be permitted to pollute stream of justice - It was bounden obligation of Court to neutralize any unjust and/or undeserved benefit oradvantage obtained by abusing judicial process - Watchman, caretaker or a servant employed to look after property could never acquire interest in property irrespective of his long possession - Watchman, caretaker or a servant was under an obligation to hand over possession forthwith on demand - With regard to principles of justice, equity and good conscience, Courts were not justified in protecting possession of a watchman, caretaker or servant who was only allowed to live into premises to look after same - Watchman, caretaker or agent held property of principal only on behalf principal - He acquired no right or interest whatsoever in such property irrespective of his long stay or possession - Protection of Court could be granted or extended to person who had valid subsisting rent agreement, lease agreement or licence agreement in his favour - Appellant directed to vacate premises and handover peaceful possession of suit property to Respondent-Society - Appeals dismissed

Facts:

These two appeals arise out of cross suits filed before the High Court of Judicature at Madras in S.A. No. 1973 of 2002 and S.A. No. 869 of 2009 dated April 20, 2011. In both these appeals, A. Shanmugam is the Appellant and Ariya Kshatriya Raja Kulavamsa Madalaya Nandhavana Paripalana Sangam is the Respondent which for convenience hereinafter is referred to as the 'Society'.

1. The property in question belonged to one, Muthu Naicker, who dedicated the suit land for construction of a Dharamshala. In the southern part of India, it is called as 'choultry'. A 'Dharamshala' is commonly known as 'a place where boarding facilities are provided either free of cost or at a nominal cost'. In the instant case, a Dharamshala was to be constructed for the benefit of the Ariya Kshatriya community. The Appellant's father, Appadurai Pillai was engaged as a Watchman on a monthly salary by the Respondent-Society to look after the Dharamshala and in that capacity lived in the premises with his family including the Appellant.

2. According to the Appellant, in the year 1994, the Respondent-Society claiming to be the owner of the suit property tried to dispossess the Appellant by force necessitating the Appellant to file a suit in O.S. No. 1143

of 1994 on the file of the Second Additional District Munsif, Tiruvannamalai praying for issuance of permanent injunction against the Respondent-Society. The said suit was, however, dismissed. As against that, the Appellant preferred an appeal in A.S. No. 94 of 2001 on the file of the Additional District Judge, Tiruvannamalai and the said appeal was allowed and consequently, the Appellant's suit was decreed. The Respondent-Society preferred a Second Appeal in S.A. No. 1973 of 2002 before the High Court of Madras against the said judgment of the Additional District Judge.

3. The Respondent-Society during the pendency of Second Appeal filed a suit in O.S. No. 239 of 2003 before the Additional Subordinate Judge, Tiruvannamalai praying for declaration of title and recovery of possession of the suit property comprised in T.S. No. 1646/1 of Tiruvannamalai Town having an extent of 70 feet east to west and 30 feet north to south bearing Old Door No. 116 and New Door No. 65. The said suit was decreed as prayed for. Against that, the Appellant preferred an appeal in A.S. No. 19 of 2008 on the file of the Additional District Judge, Tiruvannamalai and the decision of the trial court was reversed in Appeal resulting in the dismissal of the suit filed by the Respondent-Society. Aggrieved against the appeal being allowed and the suit being dismissed, the Respondent-Society preferred a Second Appeal in S.A. No. 869 of 2009 before the High Court of Madras. The learned Judge of the Madras High Court heard both the aforesaid Second Appeals together and by a common judgment set aside the well-considered judgments of the First Appellate Court. Aggrieved by the said common impugned judgment, the Appellant has preferred these appeals by way of special leave.

Held by Hon'ble Supreme Court:

1. False averments of facts and untenable contentions are serious problems faced by our courts. The other problem is that litigants deliberately create confusion by introducing irrelevant and minimally relevant facts and documents. The court cannot reject such claims, defences and pleas at the first look. It may take quite sometime, at times years, before the court is able to see through, discern and reach to the truth. More often than not, they appear attractive at first blush and only on a deeper examination the irrelevance and hollowness of those pleadings and documents come to light.

2. Our courts are usually short of time because of huge pendency of cases and at times the courts arrive at an erroneous conclusion because of false pleas, claims, defences and irrelevant facts. A litigant could deviate from the

facts which are liable for all the conclusions. In the journey of discovering the truth, at times, this Court, on later stage, but once discovered, it is the duty of the Court to take appropriate remedial and preventive steps so that noone should derive benefits or advantages by abusing the process of law. The court must effectively discourage fraudulent and dishonest litigants.

3. Now, when we revert to the facts of this case it becomes quite evident that the Appellant is guilty of suppressing material facts and introducing false pleas and irrelevant documents. The Appellant has also clouded the entire case with pleas which have nothing to do with the main controversy involved in the case.

IRRELEVANT DOCUMENTS:

4. All documents filed by the Appellant along with the plaint have no relevance to the controversy involved in the case. We have reproduced a list of the documents to demonstrate that these documents have been filed to mislead the Court. The First Appellate Court has, in fact, got into the trap and was misled by the documents and reached to an entirely erroneous finding that resulted in undue delay of disposal of a small case for almost 17 years.

FALSE and IRRELEVANT PLEAS:

5. The Appellant is also guilty of introducing untenable pleas. The plea of adverse possession which has no foundation or basis in the facts and circumstances of the case was introduced to gain undue benefit. The Court must be cautious in granting relief to a party guilty of deliberately introducing irrelevant and untenable pleas responsible for creating unnecessary confusion by introducing such documents and pleas. These factors must be taken into consideration while granting relief and/or imposing the costs.

6. On the facts of the present case, following principles emerge:

1. It is the bounden duty of the Court to uphold the truth and do justice.

2. Every litigant is expected to state truth before the law court whether it is pleadings, affidavits or evidence. Dishonest and unscrupulous litigants have no place in law courts.

3. The ultimate object of the judicial proceedings is to discern the truth and do justice. It is imperative that pleadings and all other presentations before the court should be truthful.

4. Once the court discovers falsehood, concealment, distortion, obstruction or confusion in pleadings and documents, the court should in addition to full restitution impose appropriate costs. The court must ensure

that there is no incentive for wrong doer in the temple of justice. Truth is the foundation of justice and it has to be the common endeavour of all to uphold the truth and no one should be permitted to pollute the stream of justice.

5. It is the bounden obligation of the Court to neutralize any unjust and/or undeserved benefit or advantage obtained by abusing the judicial process.

6. Watchman, caretaker or a servant employed to look after the property can never acquire interest in the property irrespective of his long possession. The watchman, caretaker or a servant is under an obligation to hand over the possession forthwith on demand. According to the principles of justice, equity and good conscience, Courts are not justified in protecting the possession of a watchman, caretaker or servant who was only allowed to live into the premises to look after the same.

7. The watchman, caretaker or agent holds the property of the principal only on behalf the principal. He acquires no right or interest whatsoever in such property irrespective of his long stay or possession.

8. The protection of the Court can be granted or extended to the person who has valid subsisting rent agreement, lease agreement or licence agreement in his favour.

7. In the instant case, we would have ordinarily imposed heavy costs and would have ordered restitution but looking to the fact that the Appellant is a Watchman and may not be able to bear the financial burden, we dismiss these appeals with very nominal costs of Rs. 25,000/- to be paid within a period of two months and direct the Appellant to vacate the premises within two months from today and handover peaceful possession of the suit property to the Respondent-Society. In case, the Appellant does not vacate the premises within two months from today, the Respondent-Society would be a liberty to take police help and get the premises vacated.

8. Both the appeals are, accordingly dismissed, leaving the parties to bear their own costs.

Pushpalata vs. Vijay Kumar (Dead) thr. L.Rs. and Ors. (05.09.2022 - SC) : MANU/ SC/1101/2022

Relative Section:

Code of Civil Procedure, 1908 (CPC) - Section 100;

Constitution of India - Article 136;

Prohibition Of Benami Property Transactions Act, 1988 - Section 2,
Prohibition Of Benami Property Transactions Act, 1988 - Section 3,
Prohibition Of Benami Property Transactions Act, 1988 - Section 4,
Prohibition Of Benami Property Transactions Act, 1988 - Section 4(1),
Prohibition Of Benami Property Transactions Act, 1988 - Section 4(3)

Hon'bleJudges/Coram:

U.U. Lalit, C.J.I., S. Ravindra Bhat and Sudhanshu Dhulia

Equivalent Citation: AIR2022SC4118, 2022(5)ALD300, 2022(5)ALT78, 2022(5)BomCR514, 2022 (3) CCC 297 , 2022(4)CivilCC(S.C.), 2023(1)ICC212, 2022/INSC/908, 2022(4)J.L.J.R.205, 2022(5)KLT653, 2023(1)MhLj633, 2023(1)MPLJ305, 2023(1)MPLJ305, 2022(4)PLJR263, 2022(4)RCR(Civil)267

Case Reference:

Valliammal (D) by Lrs. v. Subramaniam and Ors. MANU/SC/0699/ 2004;

R. Rajagopal Reddy (Dead) by L.Rs. and Ors. v. Padmini Chandrasekharan (Dead) by L.Rs. MANU/SC /0061 /1996;

Binapani Paul v. Pratima Ghosh and Ors. MANU/SC/2428/2007;

Jaydayal Poddar (Deceased) through L.Rs. and Ors. v. Bibi Hazra and Ors. MANU/SC/0332/1973;

Krishnanand v. The State of Madhya Pradesh MANU/SC/0134/1976;

Thakur Bhim Singh (Dead) by Lrs and Ors. v. Thakur Kan Singh MANU/SC/0516/1979;

His Highness Maharaja Pratap Singh v. Her Highness Maharani Sarojini Devi and Ors. MANU/SC/0963/1994; Heirs of Vrajlal J. Ganatra v. Heirs of Parshottam S. Shah MANU/SC/1161/1996;

Marcel Martins v. M. Printer and Ors. MANU/SC/0333/2012;

Collector Singh v. L.M.L. Ltd. MANU/SC/1005/2014;

Nizam and Ors. v. State of Rajasthan MANU/SC/0964/2015

NumberofPagesintheOriginalJudgment:11

Case Note:

Civil - Benami ownership - Existence of - Section 4(3)(a) of Benami Transaction Act, 1988- Plaintiff purchased property in name of first Defendant-son - As per plaintiff, properties were bought by him for proper maintenance and education of his children - First defendant sold land to third Defendant (purchaser) - Plaintiff filed suit seeking setting aside of sale deed and relief of declaration of title - Plaintiffs urged that first Defendant was benami owner who could not have alienated suit property - Trial Court dismissed suit on ground that original Plaintiff had failed to prove that suit property was purchased for welfare of coparceners of HUF - Appellate court declined Plaintiffs' appeal holding that Plaintiff himself intended for first Defendant to be absolute owner, and it was not benami transaction - High Court dismissed second appeal by reiterating that Plaintiffs had failed to prove that property was purchased for benefit of coparceners - Hence, present appeal - Whether elements necessary to establish benami ownership within meaning of Section 4(3)(a) of Act had been satisfied by first Plaintiff.

Facts:

The original first Plaintiff purchased a property in the name of first Defendant-son. It was alleged that Laxmi Prasad later constructed a two-storied building, with his earnings. According to plaintiff, these properties were bought by him for the proper maintenance and education of his children; he was involved in the construction business. First Defendant sold land to the third Defendant (purchaser). Plaintiff filed a suit seeking setting aside of the sale deed and the relief of declaration of title. The Plaintiffs urged that they and the first and second Defendants, were members of a

HUF, and that original first Defendant was a benami owner who could not have alienated the suit property. The trial court dismissed the suit on the ground that the original Plaintiff had failed to prove by cogent evidence that the suit property was purchased for the welfare of the coparceners of the HUF and declared that the first Defendant had the right to sell the disputed properties in his name. The appellate court declined the Plaintiffs' appeal holding that the first Plaintiff himself intended for the first Defendant to be the absolute owner, and it was not a benami transaction. The High Court by impugned judgment dismissed the second appeal, with costs. The High Court reiterated that the Plaintiffs had failed to prove that the property was purchased for the benefit of the coparceners, and hence the suit was rightly rejected as not maintainable.

Held, while allowing the appeal:

(i) There was nothing on the record, to support the plea of first Defendant that he was the real and true owner of the property. The trial and first appellate court had not relied on any material to show that first defendant had any source of income, or was living away from his father, or was not dependant on him. The faint suggestion that first defendant's maternal grandparents had lent the money, was denied by the Plaintiff; no defence witness in support of that suggestion appears to have been examined. [18]

(ii) The first Defendant, and those claiming through him, as subsequent purchasers, did not lead any evidence to show that the first Defendant had the means or any source of income, to purchase the property, quite apart from the fact that he was a dependent of plaintiff, and minor at the time of acquisition of the properties. Furthermore, the first Defendant also made inconsistent pleas-apart from asserting that he was owner of the property he alleged to have perfected title, through adverse possession, a plea which he did not support during the evidence. This was fatal to his case, further, the written statement was bereft of any details as regards the date from when he claimed hostile possession, against his father. [25]

(iii) The High Court fell into error, in ignoring that the circumstances of this case, where the first Plaintiff had proved that the properties had been purchased, with his funds, and the sons were minors, with no source of income. The second Defendant's position-throughout all the proceedings, was that the properties were that of the first Plaintiff, in other words, he admitted to the suit averments. The Plaintiff also proved that he had possession of the property, by adducing positive evidence of tenants, who paid rent to him. In these circumstances, the elements necessary to establish benami ownership within the meaning of Section 4(3)(a) of the Act, in terms of the judgments in Binapani Paul and Valliammal had been satisfied by the first Plaintiff. [29]

Disposition:

Appeal Allowed

Ravinder Kaur Grewal and Ors. vs. Manjit Kaur and Ors. (07.08.2019 - SC) : MANU/SC/1053/2019

Relative Section:

Code of Civil Procedure, 1908 (CPC) - Section 66,Section 96, Section 100;

Indian Limitation Act, 1908 - Schedule - Article 134B, Article 142, Article 144; Section 28;

Limitation Act, 1963 - Section 10,Section 27;

Limitation Act, 1963 - Schedule - Article 64,

Limitation Act, 1963 - Schedule - Article 65;

Specific Relief Act 1963 - Section 6, Section 9

Hon'bleJudges/Coram:

Arun Mishra, S. Abdul Nazeer and M.R. Shah

Equivalent Citation: 2019(6)ABR57, 2020(206)AIC75, AIR2019SC3827, 2019(5)ALD243, 2020 (139) ALR 717, 2019(5)ALT38, 2019 6 AWC5239SC, 2019(5)BLJ151, 2019 (3) CCC 171 , 2019(5) CHN (SC) 136, 2019(4)CivilCC(S.C.), 2019(1)CivilCC(S.C.), 2019(4)CTC936, 2019(II)CLR(SC)437, 262(2019)DLT1, 2019GLH(3)436, ILR2019(3)Kerala599, 2019/INSC/869, 2019(3)J.L.J.R.459, 2020(4)JKJ244[SC], 2019(3)JLJ481, 2019 (4) KHC 256, 2019(3)KLT865, 2020-2-LW207, 2019(6)MhLj87, (2019)6MLJ96, 2019(4)MPLJ196, 2019(II)OLR478, 2019(3)PLJR420, 2019(4)RCR(Civil)1, 2020 148 RD208, 2019(3)RLW2255(SC), 2019(10)SCALE473, (2019)8SCC729, 2019 (8)

SCJ 694, [2019]11SCR74, (2020)1WBLR(SC)101

Case Reference:

Gurudwara Sahib v. Gram Panchayat Village Sirthala and Anr. MANU/SC/0939/2013; Gurdwara Sahib v. State of Punjab and Ors. MANU/PH/0366/2009;

Sri Sarangadevar Peria Matam and Anr. v. Ramaswamy Gounder (Dead) by Legal Representatives MANU/SC/0257/1965;

Babajirao Gambhirsing v. Laxmandas Guru Raghunathdas MANU/MH/0042/1903; Balkrishan v. Satyaprakash and Ors. MANU/SC/0043/2001;

Des Raj and Ors. v. Bhagat Ram (Dead) By LRs. and Ors. MANU/SC/7153/2007; Govindammal v. R. Perumal Chettiar and Ors. MANU/SC/8567/2006;

Kshitish Chandra Bose v. Commissioner of Ranchi MANU/SC/0364/1981;

Nair Service Society Ltd. v. Rev. Fr. K.C. Alexander MANU/SC/0144/1968;

Midnapur Zamindari Company Ld. v. Naresh Narayan Roy MANU/PR/0054/1920;

Yar Muhammad and Anr. v. Lakshmi Das and Ors. MANU/UP/0001/1959;

Somnath Burman v. Dr. S.P. Raju and Anr. MANU/SC/0399/1969;

Ajudhia Kandu v. Wali Ahmad Khan and Others MANU/UP/0034/1891;

Subodh Gopal Bose v. Province of Bihar and Ors. MANU/BH/0055/1950;

Padmini Bai v. Tangavva and Ors. MANU/SC/0385/1979;

State of West Bengal v. The Dalhousie Institute Society MANU/SC/0447/1970;

Hafiz Mohammed Fateh Nasib v. Sir Swarup Chand Hukum Chand, a firm and Anr. MANU/PR/0021/1947;

S.M. Karim v. Mst. Bibi Sakina MANU/SC/0236/1964;

Sribhagwan Singh and Ors. v. Rambasi Kuer and Ors. MANU/BH/0054/1957;

Bishun Dayal v. Kesho Prasad and Anr. MANU/PR/0042/1940;

Mandal Revenue Officer v. Goundla Venkaiah and Anr. MANU/SC/0026/2010;

State of Rajasthan v. Harphool Singh (Dead) Through His L.Rs. MANU/SC/0348/2000; Annakili v. A. Vedanayagam and Ors. MANU/SC/8027/2007;

P.T. Munichikkanna Reddy and Ors. v. Revamma and Ors. MANU/SC/7325/2007;

P. Lakshmi Reddy v. L. Lakshmi Reddy MANU/SC/0083/1956;

State of Haryana v. Mukesh Kumar and Ors. MANU/SC/1147/2011;

Krishnamurthy S. Setlur Dead by LRs. v. O.V. Narasimha Setty and Ors. MANU/SC/1169/2007;

Lala Hem Chand v. Lala Pearey Lal and others MANU/PR/0031/1942;

Ram Daan v. Urban Improvement Trust MANU/SC/0675/2014;

Aboobucker s/o Shakhi Mahomed Laloo and others v. Sahibkhatoon and others MANU/SN/0056/1947;

Rangappa Nayakar v. Rangaswami Nayakar and Ors. MANU/TN/0574/1924;

Pannalal Bhagirath Marwadi v. Bhaiyalal Bindraban Pardeshi MANU/NA/0090/1936; Krishna Ram Mahale (Dead), by his Lrs. v. Mrs. Shobha Venkat Rao MANU/SC/0278/1989;

State of Uttar Pradesh and Ors. v. Maharaja Dharmander Prasad Singh and Ors. MANU/SC/0563/1989;

Hemaji Waghaji Jat v. Bhikhabhai Khengarbhai Harijan and Ors. MANU/SC/4083/2008;

T. Anjanappa and Ors. v. Somalingappa and Anr. MANU/SC/8429/2006;

State of Uttarakhand and Ors. v. Mandir Sri Laxman Sidh Maharaj MANU/SC/1180/2017;

Dharampal (dead) thr. L.Rs. v. Punjab Wakf Board and Ors. MANU/SC/1204/2017; State of Rajasthan & Anr. v. M/s Mahaveer Oil Industries & Ors. MANU/SC/0292/1999;

Director of Settlements, Andhra Pradesh and Ors. v. M.R. Apparao and Anr. MANU/SC/0219/2002;

Uptron India Limited v. Shammi Bhan & Anr. MANU/SC/0258/1998;

Musumut Chundrabullee Debia v. Luchea Debia Chowdrain MANU/PR/0005/1865; Mahadeo Prasad Singh v. Karia Bharti MANU/PR/0051/1934 : 62 Ind App 47; Vithalbowa v. Narayan Daji, (1893) I.L.R. 18 Bom 507;

Sk. Mukbool Ali v. Sk. Wajed Hossein, (1876) 25 WR 249;

Burling v. Read (1848) 11 QB 904;

Lallu Yashwant Singh (dead) by his legal representative v. Rao Jagdish Singh and Ors. MANU/SC/0425/1967 :

AIR 1968 SC 620; K.K. Verma v. Naraindas C. Malkani AIR 1954 Bom 358;

Wali Ahmad Khan v. Ayodhya Kundu MANU/UP/0034/1891 : (1891)

ILR 13 All. 537; Hillava Subbava v. Narayanappa MANU/MH/0143/1911 : (1911) 13 Bom.

LR 1200; Lillu v. Annaji (1881) ILR 5 Bom. 387; Bandu v. Naba (1890) ILR 15 Bom 238;

Narayana Row v. Dharmachar, MANU/TN/0088/1902 : (1903) ILR 26 Mad 514;

Krishnarao Yashwant v. Vasudev Apaji Ghotikar, (1884) ILR 8 Bom 871;

Umrao Singh v. Ramji Das, MANU/UP/0015/1913 : ILR 36 All 51;

Debi Churn Boldo v. Issur Chunder Manjee, MANU/WB/0131/1882 : (1883) ILR 9 Cal 39;

Ertaza Hossein v. Bany Mistry, MANU/WB/0156/1882 : (1883) ILR 9 Cal 130; Purmeshur Chowdhry v. Brijo Lall Chowdhry, MANU/WB/0114/1889 : (1890) ILR 17 Cal 256;

Nisa Chand Gaita v. Kanchiram Bagani, MANU/WB/0277/1899 : (1899) ILR 26 Cal 579;

Bombay v. Municipal Corporation of the City of Bombay, MANU/SC/0001/1951 : [1952] SCR 43;

Gunga Govind Mundul and Ors. v. The Collector of the Twenty-Four Pergunnahs and Ors. MANU/PR/0010/1867 : 11 M.I.A. 212;

Sukhan Das v. Krishanand, ILR 32 Pat 353;

Fairweather v. St Marylebone Property Co. Ltd. MANU/UKHL/0001/1962 : (1962) 2 All ER 288 (HL);

Taylor v. Twinberrow (1930) 2 K.B. 16: 1930 All ER Rep 342 (DC);

Downing v. Bird 100 So. 2d 57 (Fla. 1958);

Arkansas Commemorative Commission v. City of Little Rock 227 Ark. 1085: 303 S.W. 2d 569 (1957);

Monnot v. Murphy 207 N.Y. 240 100 N.E. 742 (1913);

City of Rock Springs v. Sturm 39 Wyo. 494: 273 P. 908: 97 A.L.R. 1 (1929);

Toltec Ranch Co. v. Cook, MANU/USSC/0073/1903 : 191 U.S. 532(1903);

Field v. Peoples, 180 Ill. 376, 383 : 54 N.E. 304 (1899); Bellefontaine Co. v. Niedringhaus, 181 Ill. 426 : 55 N.E. 184 (1899);

Cf. La Salle v. Sanitary District, 260 Ill. 423 : 103 N.E. 175 (1913);

Camp v. Camp, 5 Conn. 291 (1824); Price v. Lyon, 14 Conn. Conn. 279, 290 (1841); Coal Creek, etc. Co. v. East Tenn. I. & C. Co., 105 Tenn. 563 : 59 S.W. 634 (1900); Gunga Gobindas Mundal v. The Collector of the Twenty Four Pergunnahs MANU/PR/0010/1867 : 11 M.I.A. 345: 7 W.R. 21:

1 Suther. 676: 2 Sar. 284 (P.C.); Tichborne v. Weir, (1892) 67 LT 735; Perry v. Clissold 1907 AC 73 (PC);

Nepen Bala Debi v. Siti Kanta Banerjee, MANU/WB/0587/1910 : (1910) 8 Ind Cas 41 (DB) (Cal);

Ngasepam Ibotombi Singh v. Wahengbam Ibohal Singh and Anr. AIR 1960 Manipur 16;

Bata Krista Pramanick v. Shebaits of Thakur Jogendra Nath Maity and Ors. MANU/WB/0139/1919 : AIR 1919 Cal. 339;

Ram Chandra Sil and Ors. v. Ramanmani Dasi and Ors. MANU/WB/0495/1916 : AIR 1917 Cal. 469;

Shiromani Gurdwara Parbhandhak Committee, Khosakotla and Anr. v. Prem Das and Ors. MANU/LA/0522/1932 : AIR 1933 Lah 25;

Radhamoni Debi v. The Collector of Khulna and Ors. MANU/WB/0070/1900 : (1900) ILR 27 Cal. 943;

Gurdwara Sahib Sannauli v. State of Punjab MANU/PH/0366/2009 : (2009) 154 PLR 756;

Bachhaj Nahar v. Nillima Mandal and Anr. MANU/SC/8199/2008 : J.T. 2008 (13) S.C. 255;

Bhim Singh and Ors. v.Zile Singh and Ors., MANU/PH/0354/2006 :(2006) 3 RCR Civil 97:AIR 2006 P & H 195;

State of Haryana v. Mukesh Kumar and Ors. MANU/PH/0364/2009 : (2009) 154 P.L.R. 753;

Prem Nath Wadhawan v. Inder Rai Wadhawan MANU/DE/0842/1993 : 1993 3 105 PLR (Delhi Section) 70;

Parsinni v. Sukhi; D.N. Venkatarayappa v. State of Karnataka;

Shaikh Alimuddin v. Shaikh Salim 1928 IC 81 (PC)

NumberofPagesintheOriginalJudgment: 36

Case Note:

Property - Adverse possession - Article 65 and Section 27 of the Limitation Act, 1963 - Issue in present case regarding plea of acquisition of title by adverse possession by Plaintiff under Article 65 of the Limitation Act - Whether Article 65 of the Act only enabled a person to set up a plea of adverse possession as a shield as a Defendant and such a plea could not be used as a sword by a Plaintiff to protect possession of immovable property or to recover it in case of dispossession - Whether he was remediless in such a case - In case a person had perfected his title based on adverse possession and property was sold by the owner after extinguishment of his title, what was remedy of a person to avoid sale and interference in possession or for its restoration in case of dispossession.

Facts:

The question of law involved in present matters is significant. Issue is relating to nature of right acquired by adverse possession and even otherwise as to the right to protect possession against unlawful dispossession of the Plaintiff or for its recovery in case of illegal dispossession.

Held, while placing matters for consideration on merits before the appropriate Bench

1. The statute does not define adverse possession, it is a common law concept, the period of which has been prescribed statutorily under the law of limitation Article 65 as 12 years. Law of limitation does not define the concept of adverse possession nor anywhere contains a provision that the Plaintiff cannot sue based on adverse possession. It only deals with limitation to sue and extinguishment of rights. There may be a case where a person who has perfected his title by virtue of adverse possession is sought to be ousted or has been dispossessed by a forceful entry by the owner or by some other person, his right to obtain possession can be resisted only when the person who is seeking to protect his possession, is able to show that he has also perfected his title by adverse possession for requisite period against such a Plaintiff. [48]

2. Under Article 64 also, suit can be filed based on the possessory title. Law never intends a person who has perfected title to be deprived of filing suit under Article 65 to recover possession and to render him remediless. In case of infringement of any other right attracting any other Article such as in case the land is sold away by the owner after the extinguishment of his title, the suit can be filed by a person who has perfected his title by adverse possession to question alienation and attempt of dispossession. [49]

3. Law of adverse possession does not qualify only a Defendant for the acquisition of title by way of adverse possession, it may be perfected by a person who is filing a suit. It only restricts a right of the owner to recover possession before the period of limitation fixed for the extinction of his rights expires. Once right is extinguished another person acquires prescriptive right which cannot be defeated by re-entry by the owner or subsequent acknowledgment of his rights. In such a case suit can be filed by a person whose right is sought to be defeated. [50]

4. There is the acquisition of title in favour of Plaintiff though it is negative conferral of right on extinguishment of the right of an owner of

the property. The right ripened by prescription by his adverse possession is absolute and on dispossession, he can sue based on 'title' as envisaged in the opening part under Article 65 of Act. Under Article 65, the suit can be filed based on the title for recovery of possession within 12 years of the start of adverse possession, if any, set up by the Defendant. Otherwise right to recover possession based on the title is absolute irrespective of limitation in the absence of adverse possession by the Defendant for 12 years. The possession as trespasser is not adverse nor long possession is synonym with adverse possession. [53]

5. In Article 65 in the opening part a suit "for possession of immovable property or any interest therein based on title" has been used. Expression "title" would include the title acquired by the Plaintiff by way of adverse possession. The title is perfected by adverse possession has been held in a catena of decisions. [54]

6. Section 27 of Limitation Act, 1963 provides for extinguishment of right on the lapse of limitation fixed to institute a suit for possession of any property, the right to such property shall stand extinguished. The concept of adverse possession as evolved goes beyond it on completion of period and extinguishment of right confers the same right on the possessor, which has been extinguished and not more than that. For a person to sue for possession would indicate that right has accrued to him in presenti to obtain it, not in future. Any property in Section 27 would include corporeal or incorporeal property. Article 65 deals with immovable property. [55]

7. Possession is the root of title and is right like the property. As ownership is also of different kinds of viz. sole ownership, contingent ownership, corporeal ownership, and legal equitable ownership. Limited ownership or limited right to property may be enjoyed by a holder. What can be prescribable against is limited to the rights of the holder. Possession confers enforceable right under Section 6 of the Specific Relief Act. It has to be looked into what kind of possession is enjoyed viz. de facto i.e., actual, 'de jure possession', constructive possession, concurrent possession over a small portion of the property. In case the owner is in symbolic possession, there is no dispossession, there can be formal, exclusive or joint possession. The joint possessor/co-owner possession is not presumed to be adverse. Personal law also plays a role to construe nature of possession. [56]

8. The adverse possession requires all the three classic requirements to co-exist at the same time, namely, nec-vi i.e. adequate in continuity, nec-clam i.e., adequate in publicity and nec-precario i.e. adverse to a competitor,

in denial of title and his knowledge. Visible, notorious and peaceful so that if the owner does not take care to know notorious facts, knowledge is attributed to him on the basis that but for due diligence he would have known it. Adverse possession cannot be decreed on a title which is not pleaded. Animus possidendi under hostile colour of title is required. Trespasser's long possession is not synonym with adverse possession. Trespasser's possession is construed to be on behalf of the owner, the casual user does not constitute adverse possession. The owner can take possession from a trespasser at any point in time. Possessor looks after the property, protects it and in case of agricultural property by and the large concept is that actual tiller should own the land who works by dint of his hard labour and makes the land cultivable. The legislature in various States confers rights based on possession. [57]

9. Adverse possession is heritable and there can be tacking of adverse possession by two or more persons as the right is transmissible one. In our opinion, it confers a perfected right which cannot be defeated on re-entry except as provided in Article 65 itself. Tacking is based on the fulfillment of certain conditions, tacking maybe by possession by the purchaser, legatee or assignee, etc. so as to constitute continuity of possession, that person must be claiming through whom it is sought to be tacked, and would depend on the identity of the same property under the same right. Two distinct trespassers cannot tack their possession to constitute conferral of right by adverse possession for the prescribed period. [58]

10. A person in possession cannot be ousted by another person except by due procedure of law and once 12 years' period of adverse possession is over, even owner's right to eject him is lost and the possessory owner acquires right, title and interest possessed by the outgoing person/owner as the case may be against whom he has prescribed. In our opinion, consequence is that once the right, title or interest is acquired it can be used as a sword by the Plaintiff as well as a shield by the Defendant within ken of Article 65 of the Act and any person who has perfected title by way of adverse possession, can file a suit for restoration of possession in case of dispossession. In case of dispossession by another person by taking law in his hand a possessory suit can be maintained under Article 64, even before the ripening of title by way of adverse possession. By perfection of title on extinguishment of the owner's title, a person cannot be remediless. In case, he has been dispossessed by the owner after having lost the right by adverse possession, he can be evicted by the Plaintiff by taking the plea of adverse

possession. Similarly, any other person who might have dispossessed the Plaintiff having perfected title by way of adverse possession can also be evicted until and unless such other person has perfected title against such a Plaintiff by adverse possession. Similarly, under other Articles also in case of infringement of any of his rights, a Plaintiff who has perfected the title by adverse possession, can sue and maintain a suit. [59]

11. When law of adverse possession as has developed vis-a-vis to property dedicated to public use is considered, Courts have been loath to confer the right by adverse possession. There are instances when such properties are encroached upon and then a plea of adverse possession is raised. In such cases, on the land reserved for public utility, it is desirable that rights should not accrue. The law of adverse possession may cause harsh consequences, hence, we are constrained to observe that it would be advisable that concerning such properties dedicated to public cause, it is made clear in the statute of limitation that no rights can accrue by adverse possession. [60]

12. Resultantly, decisions of Gurudwara Sahab v. Gram Panchayat Village Sirthala and decision relying on it in State of Uttarakhand v. Mandir Shri Lakshmi Siddh Maharaj and Dharampal (dead) through LRs v. Punjab Wakf Board cannot be said to be laying down the law correctly, thus they are hereby overruled. Plea of acquisition of title by adverse possession can be taken by Plaintiff under Article 65 of the Limitation Act and there is no bar under the Limitation Act, 1963 to sue on aforesaid basis in case of infringement of any rights of a Plaintiff. [61]

CHAPTER TEN

Uttam Chand (D) through L.Rs. vs. Nathu Ram (D) through L.Rs. and Ors. (15.01.2020 - SC) : MANU/SC/0033/2020

Relative Section:

Arms Act 1959 - Section 29(b);
Limitation Act, 1963 - Schedule - Article 65

Hon'bleJudges/Coram:

L. Nageswara Rao and Hemant Gupta

Equivalent Citation:AIR2020SC461, 2020(1)ALD245, 2020(5)ALT89, 2020 (1) CCC 248 , 2020(1)CivilCC(S.C.), 2020(I)CLR(SC)656, 2020/INSC/42, 2020(1)J.L.J.R.288, 2020(3)JKJ328[SC], 2020-3-LW728, (2020)1MLJ837, 2021 (1) MWN 706, 2020(1)PLJR332, 2020(1)RCR(Civil)721, (2020)11SCC263, 2020 (2) SCJ 73, [2020]5SCR1, 2020 (1) WLN 140 (SC)

Case Reference:

T. Anjanappa and Ors. v. Somalingappa and Anr. MANU/SC/8429/2006;
Karnataka Board of Wakf v. Government of India and Ors. MANU/SC/0377/2004; Kurella Naga Druva Vudaya Bhaskara Rao v. Galla Jani Kamma Alias Nacharamma MANU/SC/7914/2008;
Dagadabai (dead) by L.Rs. v. Abbas MANU/SC/0438/2017;

Vidya Devi alias Vidya Vati (Dead by L.R's) v. Prem Prakash and others MANU/SC/0345/1995;

Annasaheb Bapusaheb Patil and others v. Balwant alias Balasaheb Babusaheb Patil (dead) by LRs. & heirs etc. MANU/SC/0172/1995;

M. Venkatesh and Ors. v. Commissioner, Bangalore Development Authority and Ors. MANU/SC/1081/2015;

Chatti Konati Rao and Ors. v. Palle Venkata Subba Rao MANU/SC/1033/2010; Ravinder Kaur Grewal and Ors. v. Manjit Kaur and Ors. MANU/SC/1053/2019;

Supdt. and Remembrancer of Legal Affairs, West Bengal v. Anil Kumar Bhunja and Ors. MANU/SC/0266/1979;

P. Lakshmi Reddy v. L. Lakshmi Reddy MANU/SC/0083/1956;

Annakili v. A. Vedanayagam and Ors. MANU/SC/8027/2007;

M Siddiq (D) through L.Rs v. Mahant Suresh Das and Ors. MANU/SC/1538/2019;

Secretary of State for India v. Debendra Lal Khan MANU/PR/0072/1933 : (1933) LR 61 IA 78;

Brijesh Kumar and Anr. v. Shardabai (Dead) by Legal Representatives and Ors. MANU/SC/1448/2019

NumberofPagesintheOriginalJudgment:9

Case Note:

Property - Possession - Plaintiff was in appeal before present Court aggrieved against judgment and decree passed by High Court whereby, Defendants second appeal was allowed and suit of Plaintiff for possession on basis of title was dismissed - Whether Defendants had perfected their title by adverse possession.

Facts:

The Plaintiff filed a suit for possession on the basis of purchase of suit property from the Managing Officer, Department of Rehabilitation, Government of India in a public auction held on 21st March, 1964. The High Court returned a finding that Tara Chand was in occupation of the suit property even prior to the purchase of the same by the Plaintiff in the year 1964. The Court referred to the judgment of this Court reported as T. Anjanappa and Ors. v. Somalingappa and Anr. to hold that the Defendants were in open, uninterrupted, peaceful and hostile possession since March, 1964 and the period of 12 years was completed in March, 1976. Therefore, the suit filed by the Plaintiff on 17th February, 1979 was barred by limitation. The Appellant argued that for a successful plea of adverse possession against the true owner, the person in possession has to admit hostile possession to the knowledge of the true owner. The Defendants in their written statement have not admitted the title of the Appellant and of adverse possession to the knowledge of the true owner. The Defendants have denied vesting of the land with the Managing Officer and the subsequent sale in favour of the Appellant. Thetrial court has returned a finding as to the title of the Appellant itself and such finding has not been set aside neither by the First Appellate Court nor by the High Court. The Defendants are asserting their long and continuous possession but such possession howsoever long cannot be termed as adverse possession so as to perfect title within the meaning of Article 65 of the Limitation Act. It was argued that long possession is not necessarily adverse possession.

Held, while allowing the appeal

1. In Kurella Naga Druva Vudaya Bhaskara Rao, the payment of tax receipts and mere possession for some years was found insufficient to claim adverse possession. It was held that if according to the Defendant, the Plaintiff was not the true owner, his possession hostile to the Plaintiff's title will not be sufficient. [12]

2. The matter has been examined by a Constitution Bench in M Siddiq (D) through L.Rs v. Mahant Suresh Das and Ors. wherein, it has been held that a plea of adverse possession is founded on the acceptance that ownership of the property vests in another, against whom the claimant asserts possession adverse to the title of the other. [15]

3. In the present case, the Defendants have not admitted the vesting of the suit property with the Managing Officer and the factum of its transfer in favour of the Plaintiff. The Defendants have denied the title not only of the Managing Officer but also of the Plaintiff. The plea of the Defendants is one of continuous possession but there is no plea that such possession was hostile to the true owner of the suit property. The evidence of the Defendants is that of continuous possession. Some of the receipts pertain to 1963 but possession since November, 1963 till the filing of the suit will not ripe into title as the Defendants never admitted the Plaintiff-Appellant to be owner or that the land ever vested with the Managing Officer. The findings recorded by the High Court that the Defendants have perfected their title by adverse possession are not legally sustainable. Consequently, the judgment and decree passed by the High Court is set aside and the suit is decreed. The appeal is allowed. [16]

Disposition:

Appeal Allowed

Shamsher Singh and Ors. vs. Nahar Singh (D) thr. L.Rs. and Ors. (29.07.2019 - SC) : MANU/SC/0986/2019

Relative Section:

Code of Civil Procedure (CPC) (Amendment) Act, 1976;

Code of Civil Procedure, 1908 (CPC) - Order XXI Rule 35,36, Rule 58,Rule 59, Rule 60,Rule 61,Rule 62,Rule 63, Rule 97,Rule 97(2), Rule 98,Rule 99, Rule 100,Rule 101,Rule 102,Rule 103,Rule 104, Rule 105,Rule 106;

Transfer of Property Act, 1882 - Section 52

Hon'bleJudges/Coram:

Ashok Bhushan and Navin Sinha

Equivalent Citation: : 2019(203)AIC173, AIR2019SC4840, 2019(4)ALD258, 2019 (137) ALR 263, 2019(5)ALT194, 2019(5)BLJ31, (2020)2CALLT33(SC), 2019(4)CivilCC(S.C.), 2019(1)CivilCC(S.C.), 128(2019)CLT985, 2019(6)CTC71, 2019(II)CLR(SC)653, 2019/INSC/820, 2019(3)J.L.J.R.397, 2020-2-LW573, 2020(2)MhLj282, 2020(1)MPLJ525, 2019(3)PLJR381, 2019(3)RCR(Civil)926, 2020 146 RD697, 2020 146 RD439, 2019(10)SCALE93, (2019)17SCC279, 2019 (7) SCJ 95, [2019]9SCR1155, 2020 (1) WLN 104 (SC)

Case Reference:

Shreenath & Another v. Rajesh & Others MANU/SC/0286/1998;

Noorduddin v. Dr K.L. Anand MANU/SC/0533/1995;

Silverline Forum Pvt. Ltd. v. Rajiv Trust and another MANU/SC/0252/
1998;

Ghasi Ram and Others v. Chait Ram Saini and Others MANU/SC/0433/
1998;

Ashan Devi and Anr. v. Phulwasi Devi and Ors. MANU/SC/0949/2003;

Bhag Mal v. Ch. Parbhu Ram and Ors. MANU/SC/0154/1984

NumberofPagesintheOriginalJudgment:14

Case Note:

Property - Title over suit premises - Proof thereto - Order XXI Rules 98,
99 and 100 of the Code of Civil Procedure, 1908 (CPC) - Present appeal
had been filed against Division Bench Judgment of High Court, by which
appeal filed by the Respondent No. 1 has been allowed setting aside order
of Executing Court rejecting application filed by Respondent No. 1 under
Order XXI Rules 98, 99 and 100 of CPC - Whether Executing Court had
rightly rejected application of Respondent No. 1 filed under Order XXI
Rules 98, 99 and 100 of CPC, he having failed to prove his title over suit
premises.

Facts:

Respondent No. 1 claimed right and title of the suit premises on the
basis of adverse possession. It was further claimed that Shamsher Singh,
Rajvindar Singh and Dayal Singh had fraudulently obtained decree in
collusion with Anadi Dutt and has evicted the Respondent No. 1 from the
suit property. Executing Court by order rejected miscellaneous case filed
by Respondent No. 1. Executing court held that, Respondent No. 1 failed
to prove that he has acquired title by way of adverse possession. Against
the order rejecting the Misc. applications filed by Respondent No. 1, first
appeal, was filed by Respondent No. 1 in High Court, which appeal has
been allowed by High Court by the impugned judgment. The High Court
by impugned judgment has set aside the order of the Executing Court
disposing the application filed by Respondent No. 1 under Order XXI Rules
98, 99 and 100 of CPC with a direction that, Appellant (Respondent No. 1
in this appeal) should be put back into possession of the suit property. Held,
while allowing the appeal

1. There is no dispute between the parties that the premises in question
was originally owned by one Tarapada Dutta. The case of the Respondent
No. 1 is that his father Late Iqbal Singh has trespassed into the premises and
after his death in 1965, it was Respondent No. 1, who was in occupation and
possession of the premises. In pursuance of decree for specific performance

of contract passed in suit, in execution proceedings, the decree holders were put in possession on 12.04.1996. At the time of taking possession, one Shri Gopal Adak was found present in the premises, who had claimed to be employee of Respondent No. 1. Respondent No. 1 had filed a suit for declaration of the title on the basis of adverse possession. [7]

2. In the application, which was filed by Respondent No. 1 for putting him back into possession under Order XXI Rules 98, 99 and 100 of CPC, the Respondent No. 1 has claimed his possession since 1965 after death of his father. There is no dispute between the parties that in execution of decree of specific performance, the Appellants were put in possession and Respondent No. 1 aggrieved by his dispossession had filed an application under Order XXI Rules 98, 99 and 100 of CPC. [8]

3. In the present case, the Rule which has fallen for interpretation is Rule 101 of Order XXI. What was the Rule 101 prior to 1976 Amendment and subsequent to 1976 amendment is relevant to be noticed to mark the difference into legislative scheme. [11]

4. Executing Court while determining the miscellaneous application of the Respondent No. 1 has considered the entire case of the Respondent No. 1 including the documents filed by him for proving his possession. The Executing Court noticed that Respondent No. 1 has already filed a Suit No. 211 of 1990 for declaration of his title on the basis of adverse possession. After considering the oral evidence and documentary evidence, the Executing Court returned the findings that Respondent No. 1 had failed to establish his case that he has clear right, title and interest over the suit property by way of adverse possession. [19]

5. The purpose of amendment under Rule 103 is also that any adjudication made under Rule 101 shall have same force and be subject to the same conditions as to an appeal or otherwise as if it was a decree. Rule 101, thus, affords an opportunity to get all issues relating to right, title or interest in the property to be determined. When the Respondent No. 1 filed his application claiming to be put back into possession, it was obliged to establish its right, title or interest in the property without which his application could not have been allowed. The Executing Court has considered the application of Respondent No. 1 in right perspective and has clearly held that Respondent No. 1 failed to prove his title by adverse possession, hence application deserves to be rejected. [27]

6. High Court committed error in observing that, in application proceedings under Order XXI Rules 99, 100 and 101, the Court is not to

decide such question. Without determination of right, title or interest, the application could not have been allowed. In the proceeding Under Order XXI Rules 99, 100 and 101, right, title or interest has to be determined and without establishing right, title or interest, the Respondent No. 1 cannot claim that he should be put back into possession. For putting back into possession, the Respondent No. 1 was obliged to establish his title to the property by adverse possession, without which, he could not have asked the Court to put him back into possession. The High Court clearly erred in allowing the appeal and the Executing Court has rightly rejected the application filed by Respondent No. 1. Suit filed by Respondent No. 1 seeking declaration of title to the property by adverse possession has been subsequently dismissed by decree and no steps have been taken for restoration of the suit. [28]

Held, while allowing the appeal

1. High Court committed error in observing that in application proceedings Under Order XXI Rules 99, 100 and 101, the Court is not to decide such question. Without determination of right, title or interest, the application could not have been allowed. We having already extracted the observations of the High Court, where it clearly held that the title in respect of the property by way of adverse possession need not be gone into in the appeal before it. The above observation of the High Court was erroneous. In the proceeding Under Order XXI Rules 99, 100 and 101, right, title or interest has to be determined and without establishing right, title or interest, the Respondent No. 1 cannot claim that he should be put back into possession. We do not accept the submission of the learned Counsel for the Respondent that on mere fact that Respondent No. 1 was in possession of the premises prior to being dispossessed, they should be put back into possession. For putting back into possession, the Respondent No. 1 was obliged to establish his title to the property by adverse possession, without which, he could not have asked the Court to put him back into possession. The High Court clearly erred in allowing the appeal and the Executing Court has rightly rejected the application filed by Respondent No. 1. We may further notice that suit No. 211 of 1990 filed by Respondent No. 1 seeking declaration of title to the property by adverse possession has been subsequently dismissed by decree on 16.03.2009 and no steps have been taken for restoration of the suit.

2. We do not find any error in the order passed by the Executing Court and the High Court committed error in allowing the appeal, directing the

Respondent No. 1 to be put back into possession. In view of the foregoing discussions, we allow this appeal and set aside the judgment of the High Court dated 15.12.2009 and restore the order of the Executing Court dated 10.08.2004. Parties shall bear their own costs.

Narasamma and Ors. vs. A. Krishnappa (26.08.2020 – SC) : MANU/SC/0610/2020

Relative Section:

Code of Civil Procedure, 1908 (CPC) - Order VII Rule 1;

Karnataka Municipal Corporation Act, 1976

Hon'bleJudges/Coram:

Sanjay Kishan Kaul, Ajay Rastogi and Aniruddha Bose

Equivalent Citation: 2020(216)AIC36, AIR2020SC4178, 2021(1) AKR 5, 2020(6)ALD60, 2021 (144) ALR 241, 2020(5)ALT188, 2021 2 AWC1527SC, 2020(5)BLJ413, 2020 (3) CCC 475 , 2021(3)CivilCC(S.C.), 2020(II)CLR(SC)577, 2021(3)ICC415, 2020/INSC/509, 2020(3)J.L.J.R.488, 2021(5)MhLj28, 2020(4)PLJR1, 2020(3)RCR(Civil)646, 2021 150 RD700, (2020)15SCC218, 2020 (7-8) SCJ 657, [2020]7SCR528

Case Reference:

Ravinder Kaur Grewal and Ors. v. Manjit Kaur and Ors. MANU/SC/ 1053/2019; Mohan Lal (Deceased) through his Lrs. Kachru and Ors. v. Mirza Abdul Gaffar and Ors. MANU/SC/1039/1996;

P.T. Munichikkanna Reddy and Ors. v. Revamma and Ors. MANU/SC/ 7325/2007;

M. Siddiq (D) thr. L.Rs. v. Mahant Suresh Das and Ors. MANU/SC/ 1538/2019;

Ram Nagina Rai and Ors. v. Deo Kumar Rai and Ors. MANU/SC/1003/ 2018; Karnataka Board of Wakf v. Government of India and Ors. MANU/ SC/0377/2004

Narasamma and Ors. vs. A. Krishnappa (26.08.2020 - SC) : MANU/SC/0610/2020

NumberofPagesintheOriginalJudgment:11

Case Note:

Property - Adverse Possession - Rights of True Owner - Suit for Possession and mesne profits - Claim resisted on the ground of continued uninterrupted possession on the basis of purported sale documents- Appellants sought to contend that the suit was barred by limitation as the induction of the original Defendant's wife was in 1976, while the suit was filed on 9.8.1989, i.e., beyond the period of twelve (12) years - Genuineness of the Agreement of Sale was not questioned, nor was the suit amended to include the prayer for cancellation of this document - On the other hand, Respondent contended that once the original Plaintiff had proved the title, the burden would shift upon the original Defendant to establish the Agreement of Sale and General Power of Attorney, or for that matter even perfection of title by adverse possession - There were concurrent findings of both the courts qua the aspect of the failure of the original Defendant to establish and prove the documents, which would show that there was no Agreement of Sale coupled with possession - Trial Court dismissed Respondent's suit - Impugned judgment reversed the finding - Hence, the present appeal

Facts:

The present issue raised the plea of adverse possession. Suit for Possession and mesne profits was filed. However, the claim was resisted on the ground the since possession remain uninterrupted on the basis of purported sale documents, ownership was absolute. - Appellants sought to contend that the suit was barred by limitation as the induction of the original Defendant's wife was in 1976, while the suit was filed on 9.8.1989, i.e., beyond the period of twelve (12) years. Trial Court dismissed Respondent's suit and Impugned judgment reversed the finding. Hence the present appeal.

Held, while rejecting the Appeal:

In order to establish adverse possession an inquiry is required to be made into the starting point of such adverse possession and, thus, when the recorded owner got dispossessed would be crucial. [34]

In the facts of the present case, the plea of adverse possession was lacking in all material particulars. [35]

The possession has to be in public and to the knowledge of the true owner as adverse, and this is necessary as a plea of adverse possession seeks to defeat the rights of the true owner. Thus, the law would not be readily accepting of such a case unless a clear and cogent basis has been made out. [36]

The legal position, thus, stands as evolved against the Appellants herein in advancing a plea of title and adverse possession simultaneously and from the same date. [38]

The appeal was held to be meritless and was accordingly dismissed with costs. [39]

Disposition:

Appeal Dismissed

Brijesh Kumar and Ors. vs. Shardabai (Dead) by L.Rs. and Ors. (01.10.2019 - SC) : MANU/SC/1448/2019

Relative Section:

Madhya Pradesh Land Revenue Code - Section 114,
Madhya Pradesh Land Revenue Code - Section 115,
Madhya Pradesh Land Revenue Code - Section 116,
Madhya Pradesh Land Revenue Code - Section 117

Hon'bleJudges/Coram:

Equivalent Citation: 2019(203)AIC7, 2019 (137) ALR 696, 2019 (4) CCC 96 , 2021(1)CTC123, ILR[2020]MP543, 2019/INSC/1104, 2019(4)JLJ369, 2020-5-LW155, (2019)7MLJ697, (2021)202PLR463, 2019(13)SCALE663, (2019)9SCC369, 2019 (10) SCJ 307, [2019]14SCR964, (2019)6WBLR(SC)427

Case Reference:

M. Venkatesh and Ors. v. Commissioner, Bangalore Development Authority and Ors. MANU/SC/1081/2015;

Dagadabai Fakirmahomed v. Sakharam Gavaji MANU/MH/0146/1946;

Wuntakal Yalpi Chenabasavana Gowd v. Rao Bahadur Y. Mahabaleshwarappa and Anr. MANU/SC/ 0117/1 954;

Mamidi Venkata Satyanarayana Manikyala Rao and Anr. v. Mandela Narasimhaswami and Ors. MANU/SC/ 0363 / 1965;

Chatti Konati Rao and Ors. v. Palle Venkata Subba Rao MANU/SC/ 1033/2010

NumberofPagesintheOriginalJudgment:6

Case Note:

Civil - Adverse possession - Denial of - Original land owners sold land to Defendant No. 9 by registered sale deed - Defendant No.9 sold particular area of land to Appellants - Plaintiff then filed Suit claiming adverse possession over suit lands relying on Khasra entries - Civil Judge decreed suit holding that Plaintiff had perfected his title by continuous, hostile and uninterrupted possession for more than twelve years adverse to that of original land owners, and that sale deeds were nullity - Civil Appeal preferred by Appellants was allowed holding that Trial court had overlooked documentary evidence on record to arrive at erroneous conclusion of adverse possession on basis of oral evidence only - Second appeal by Plaintiff was subsequently allowed holding that conclusions of first appellate court were erroneous, restoring order decreeing suit - Hence, present appeal - Whether Plaintiff acquired title by adverse possession.

Facts:

The Original land owners sold land to Defendant No. 9 by registered sale deed. By two separate registered sale deeds she sold an area to the Appellants in both the appeals. Possession was handed over and constructions raised by them. The Plaintiff then filed Suit claiming adverse possession over the suit lands relying on Khasra entries. The Plaintiff also sought a declaration of nullity against the sale deeds executed by the original land owners and subsequent thereto. The Civil Judge decreed the suit holding that the Plaintiff had perfected his title by continuous, hostile and uninterrupted possession for more than twelve years adverse to that of the original land owners, and that the sale deeds were a nullity. Regular Civil Appeal preferred by the Appellants was allowed holding that the Trial court had overlooked documentary evidence on record to arrive at an erroneous conclusion of adverse possession on basis of oral evidence only. The second appeal by the Plaintiff was subsequently allowed by the impugned order holding that the conclusions of the first appellate court were erroneous, restoring the order decreeing the suit.

Held, while allowing the appeal:

(i) The Plaintiff in a suit filed, asserted possession of the lands for past thirty years prior to the filing of the suit, relying on the Khasra entries as the foundation of the claim to adverse possession. The nature and origin of the claim for possession was absent in the pleadings. In his evidence the Respondent deposed that since the original land owner had failed to return his bullocks and agricultural equipments borrowed, he had taken possession of the lands. The original Plaintiff expired. The Respondents, who were his legal heirs, then filed an application to amend the pleadings to bring it in accord with the evidence. If the Plaintiff's possession itself originated it was difficult to appreciate how the Khasra entries in its name came to be made in the very same year. Section 115 of the Code provides that if the Tehsildar finds that a wrong or incorrect entry had been made in the land records prepared under Section 114 by an officer subordinate to him, he shall direct necessary changes to be made therein in red ink after making such enquiry from the person concerned as he may deem fit after due notice. The Plaintiff led no evidence whatsoever when the application for correction in the khasra entry was made and that the original land owner was heard before the corrections were made. The entries in the name of the purchaser pursuant to the sale deed were in blue ink. The corrections in the khasra entry, the sheet anchor of the Respondents claim therefore remains unexplained and doubtful. [6]

(ii) The High Court in second appeal arrived at a perverse finding on the evidence that Defendant No.9 never acquired possession and thus the Plaintiff had established adverse possession after twelve years. The report of the court commissioner also finds no discussion by the High Court. It also failed to deal with the suspicious Khasra entries in red ink, claimed by the Plaintiff in proof of possession. Likewise, it did not consider that the origin of the claim of the Plaintiff itself never stood established in absence of necessary pleadings which was sought to be introduced after the Plaintiff's evidence, as an afterthought. [11]

(iii) Adverse possession is hostile possession by assertion of a hostile title in denial of the title of the true owner as held in case of M. Venkatesh. The Respondent had failed to establish peaceful, open and continuous possession demonstrating a wrongful ouster of the rightful owner. It thus involved question of facts and law. The onus lay on the Respondent to establish when and how he came into possession, the nature of his possession, the factum of possession known and hostile to the other parties, continuous possession over twelve years which was open and undisturbed. The Respondent was seeking to deny the rights of the true owner. The onus therefore lay upon the Respondent to establish possession as a fact coupled with that it was open, hostile and continuous to the knowledge of the true owner. The Respondent-Plaintiff failed to discharge the onus. [13]

Disposition:

Appeal Allowed

• 62 •

Krishnamurthy S. Setlur (D) by L.Rs. vs. O.V. Narasimha Setty (D) by L.Rs. (26.09.2019 - SC) : MANU/SC/1331/2019

Relative Section:

Limitation Act, 1963 - Schedule - Article 64,

Limitation Act, 1963 - Schedule - Article 65

Hon'bleJudges/Coram:

Deepak Gupta and Aniruddha Bose

Equivalent Citation: 2019(6)ALD42, 2019(5)ALT382, 2019(6)BLJ1, 2019(1)CivilCC(S.C.), 2019(4)CivilCC(S.C.), 2020(I)CLR(SC)143, 2019/INSC/1084, 2019(4)RCR(Civil)682, 2019(13)SCALE84, (2019)9SCC488, 2019 (10) SCJ 224, (2020)1WBLR(SC)89

Case Reference:

Ravinder Kaur Grewal and Ors. v. Manjit Kaur and Ors. Civil Appeal No. 7764 of 2014

NumberofPagesintheOriginalJudgment: 7

Case Note:

Property - Possession - Issue in present case was relating to title by adverse possession in fact of present case - Whether High Court gravely erred in coming to conclusion that, KS was not in possession of suit property, when suit was filed.

Facts:

Krishnamurthy S. Setlur ('KS'), was the predecessor-in-interest of the Appellants. He was a very rich landlord. H.R. Narayana Iyengar ('HR'), was the predecessor-in-interest of the contesting Respondents. It appears that HR used to manage the properties of KS. KS had executed a general power of attorney in favour of HR to manage the properties and he used to manage and sell properties on behalf of KS. KS claimed that legal heirs of HR were illegally trying to dispossess the Plaintiff-Appellant and he sought a decree for permanent injunction. In this suit while, on the one hand, KS claimed ownership on the ground that HR was a benamidar, but in the alternative, he claimed that having been in possession of the land and having claimed ownership thereof in a manner hostile to the true owner, his possession had fructified into title by way of adverse possession. Subsequently, the suit was amended and it was pleaded that KS had been forcibly dispossessed from the land. This suit was decreed by the trial court on 11.10.1996. The trial court held that the Plaintiff-Appellant was in uninterrupted and peaceful possession of the property for over 12 years and had perfected his titled by adverse possession and it was further held that he was wrongly dispossessed by the Defendants during the pendency of the suit and, hence, decreed the suit in favour of KS. Appeal was filed by legal heirs of HR in the High Court, which was allowed on 22.03.1999. Thereafter, KS filed a special leave petition in this Court. After leave was granted, this was registered as Civil Appeal. In the said appeal, judgment of the High Court was set aside and the matter was remanded to the High Court for fresh consideration in accordance with law. After remand, the High Court again allowed the appeal vide the impugned judgment leading to present appeal.

Held, while allowing the appeal

1. High Court has not given any cogent reasons for coming to the conclusion that KS was not in possession of the property. His name figured in the revenue record from 1963 to 1981 as the owner in possession. Presumption of truth is attached to revenue record which has not been rebutted. The High Court has held, and rightly so, that in the proceedings decided in favour of KS, HR or his legal representatives were not made parties. However, the High Court lost sight of the fact that in the proceedings filed by AR, KS was not impleaded as a party though his name was shown in the revenue record. It is obvious that both sides had tried to obtain orders behind each other's back. Reliance cannot be placed on either of the documents in which all the parties were not duly represented. The net result is that KS is not the owner of the property, but it is equally true that from 1963, he had been shown to be in possession pursuant to the application (Exhibit P-10) and the order (Exhibit P-11) of the Tehsildar.

This possession was adverse to the true owner. It was openly hostile to the claim of HR and his legal representatives and they never filed a suit for possession of the property. Once it is held that KS was in possession of the suit property, the consequence will be that he is in adverse possession. The legal representatives of HR have failed to show-how they obtained possession from HR. Even, according to the case of HR, it was AR who was in possession as a tenant. AR surrendered part of the land to KS and not to HR. No doubt, in later proceedings in which KS was not a party, AR made a statement that he was never a tenant in the suit, but such statement flies in the face of the pleadings of AR in O.S. No. 79 of 1949 filed by HR and the decisions in those proceedings. Furthermore, AR had executed a registered sale-cum-release deed jointly with KS and this was ratified by the Tehsildar. [14]

2. In view of the aforesaid facts, it is apparent that the legal heirs of HR miserably failed to prove how they came into possession of the suit property. Therefore, High Court gravely erred in coming to the conclusion that KS was not in possession of the suit property when the suit was filed. He may have been dispossessed after filing of the suit but that has no effect on the case. [15]

3. In a reference made to a larger Bench of this Court in this case as well as in other connected matters in the case of Ravinder Kaur Grewal and Ors. v. Manjit Kaur and Ors., the larger Bench had held that the plea of adverse possession can be used both as an offence and as a defence i.e. both as sword and as a shield. [16]

4. Thus, there can be no manner of dispute that a Plaintiff can claim title to the property based on adverse possession. [17]

5. Judgment and decree of the High Court is set aside and that of the trial court is restored. Appeal allowed. [18]

Disposition:

Appeal Allowed

Bangalore Development Authority vs. N. Jayamma (10.03.2016 - SC) : MANU/SC/0281/2016

Relative Section:

Land Acquisition Act, 1894 [Repealed] - Section 4,

Land Acquisition Act, 1894 [Repealed] - Section 6,

Land Acquisition Act, 1894 [Repealed] - Section 16(2),

Land Acquisition Act, 1894 [Repealed] - Section 53A;

Limitation Act, 1963 - Schedule - Article 112;

Bangalore Development Authority Act, 1976 - Section 27;

Right to Fair Compensation and Transparency in Land Acquisition, Rehabilitation and Resettlement Act, 2013 - Section 24(2);

Constitution of India - Article 65,

Constitution of India - Article 136,

Constitution of India - Article 300A

Hon'bleJudges/Coram:

A.K. Sikri and R.K. Agrawal

Equivalent Citation: 2016(160)AIC48, AIR2016SC1294, 2016(2)AJR211, 2016(2) AKR 410, 2016(3) ALD119, 2016 (115) ALR 902, 2016 2 AWC2051SC, 2016(2)BLJ96, 2016 (1) CCC 208 , 2016(2) CDR313 (SC), 2016(I)CLR(SC)940, 2016/INSC/256, 2016(5)KarLJ1, (2016)3MLJ31, 2016(2)RCR(Civil)402, 2016(3) SCALE233, (2017)13SCC159, 2016 (6) SCJ 43, [2016]4SCR583

Case Reference:

M. Venkatesh and Ors. v.Commissioner, Bangalore Dev. Authority MANU/SC/1081/2015 : (2015) 10 Scale 27;

John B. James and Ors.v Bangalore Dev. Authority and Anr.MANU/KA/0046/2001:ILR 2000 KAR 4134 ;

Balwant Narayan Bhagde v. M.D. Bhagwat MANU/SC/0002/1975 : (1976) 1 SCC 700;

NTPC Ltd. v. Mahesh Dutta MANU/SC/1210/2009 : (2009) 8 SCC 339;

Raghbir Singh Sehrawat v. State of Haryana MANU/SC/1429/2011 : (2012) 1 SCC 792;

U.P. Jal Nigam v. Kalra Properties Pvt. Ltd. MANU/SC/0310/1996 : (1996) 3 SCC 124;

Ajay Kishan Singhal v. Union of India MANU/SC/0675/1996 : (1996) 10 SCC 721;

Mahavir and Anr. v. Rural Institute, Amravati and Anr. MANU/SC/0763/1995 : (1995) 5 SCC 335;

Gian Chand v. Gopala and Ors. MANU/SC/0624/1995 : (1995) 5 SCC 528;

Meera Sahni v. Lieutenant Governor of Delhi and Ors. MANU/SC/7878/2008 : (2008) 9 SCC 177;

Tika Ram v. State of Uttar Pradesh MANU/SC/1616/2009 : (2009) 10 SCC 689;

Tamil Nadu Housing Board v. A. Viswam (D) by L.Rs. (1996) 2 SCC 634;

Larsen and Toubro Ltd. v. State of Gujarat and Ors. MANU/SC/0219/1998 : (1998) 4 SCC 387;

Karnataka Board of Wakf v. Government of India MANU/SC/0377/2004 : (2004) 10 SCC 779;

S.M. Karim v. Bibi Sakina (MANU/SC/0236/1964 : AIR 1964 SC 1254;

Parsinni v. Sukhi MANU/SC/0575/1993 : (1993) 4 SCC 375;

D.N. Venkatarayappa v. State of Karnataka MANU/SC/0766/1997 : (1997) 7 SCC 567;

Mahesh Chand Sharma (Dr.) v. Raj Kumari Sharma MANU/SC/0231/1996 : (1996) 8 SCC 128;

Saroop Singh v. Banto MANU/SC/1146/2005 : (2005) 8 SCC 330;

Vasantiben Prahladji Nayak v. Somnath Muljibhai Nayak MANU/SC/0216/2004 : (2004) 3 SCC 376;

Mohd. Mohd. Ali v. Jagadish Kalita MANU/SC/0785/2003 : (2004) 1 SCC 371;

Mohan Lal v. Mirza Abdul Gaffar MANU/SC/1039/1996 : (1996) 1 SCC
639;

Annasaheb Bapusaheb Patil v. Balwant MANU/SC/0172/1995 : (1995)
2 SCC 543;

P.T. Munichikkanna Reddy and Ors. v. Revamma and Ors. MANU/SC/
7325/2007 : (2007) 6 SCC 59;

Downing v. Bird; Arkansas Commemorative Commission v. City of Little
Rock;

Monnot v. Murphy;

City of Rock Springs v. Sturm;

Rama Shankar and Anr. v. Om Prakash Likhdhari and Ors. MANU/UP/
0884/2013 : (2013) 6 ADJ 119;

East India Co. v. Oditchurn Paul

NumberofPagesintheOriginalJudgment:13

Case Note:

Limitation - Ownership by way of adverse possession - Suit filed by
Respondent - Court of City Civil Judge - Declaration of title to suit property
- Respondent claimed - Purchase of suit property from previous owner
- Constructed a building - Aforesaid suit property - Part of Scheduled
property - Acquired by State Government for Bangalore Development
Authority-Appellant - Notification Under Section 4 of Land Acquisition
Act, 1894 - Declaration Under Section 6 of the Act - Possession handed
over to BDA in 1988 - However, actual possession remained with original
owner - Original owner sold it to Respondent - Respondent filed suit for
declaration of ownership - Ground - She was in possession - More than
12 years after the acquisition by the State Government - Perfected title by
adverse possession - Trial Court decided in favour of Respondent herein -
Suit decreed in her favour - Owner in possession of suit property - Perfected
title by way of adverse possession - Decree of permanent injunction also
passed - Restrained Appellant-BDA, its officials and agents, etc. - Alienating
the suit property - Way of lease, public auction or by allotting the same
in favour of any third party - Judgment and decree appealed against by
Appellant - High Court affirmed the decree passed by trial court - Dismissed
appeal of Appellant - Present Appeal - Whether the lower courts were
correct in holding that the Respondent herein had perfected the title to
the suit schedule property by way of adverse possession - Whether the
Respondent herein have acquired and perfected their alleged title by virtue
of adverse possession - Whether the plea of equity raised by the

Respondent herein is maintainable

Facts:

The instant appeal, had its origin in a suit filed by the Respondent in the Court of City Civil Judge, Bangalore. The said suit was filed for declaration of title to the suit property situated in Sy. No. 76/1. It was claimed by the Respondent that she had purchased the property (suit property) from its previous owner and had constructed a building thereupon. The aforesaid suit property, which was part of Sy. No. 76/1 comprising 4 acres 31 guntas (scheduled property), was acquired by the State Government for Bangalore Development Authority-appellant herein (the BDA), for which Notification Under Section 4 of the Land Acquisition Act, 1894 (the Act) was issued on December 15, 1984 followed by a declaration Under Section 6 of the Act on October 29, 1986.

Purportedly, possession thereof was handed over to the BDA in 1988. However, it appears that the actual possession of the suit property remained with the original owner who then sold it to the Respondent in 1994. It is on this basis that the Respondent filed the suit on the ground that she was in possession of the said property for more than 12 years even after the acquisition thereof by the State Government and, in this manner, she had perfected her title by adverse possession. Thus, the relief claimed in the suit was for declaration that the Respondent had become the owner thereof.

The trial court decided all the issues in favour of the Respondent herein, on the basis of which suit was decreed in her favour declaring that she is the owner in possession of the suit property having perfected her title by way of adverse possession. As a consequence, decree of permanent injunction was also passed restraining the Appellant-BDA, its officials and agents, etc. from alienating the suit property either by way of lease, public auction or by allotting the same in favour of any third party or from interfering with the peaceful possession and enjoyment of the said property by the Respondent. This judgment and decree was appealed against by the Appellant before the High Court by filing Regular First Appeal. The High Court has, vide impugned judgment, affirmed the decree passed by the trial court thereby dismissing the appeal of the Appellant. Hence, the present Appeal.

Held, while allowing the appeal

1.The analysis of the judgment in M. Venkatesh and Ors. v. Commissioner, Bangalore Development Authority amply shows that it is squarely and directly applicable to the facts and circumstances of the present case. In the first instance, it shows that reliance of the Respondent herein on the judgment of John B. James and Ors. v. Bangalore Development Authority and Anr. is of no avail. It would further demonstrate that the findings of the court below that only paper possession was taken and actual possession was not taken also becomes meaningless as the manner of taking possession in the instant case was also identical. In addition, it is pertinent that the Respondent herein, in para 10 of the plaint, had herself admitted that the officials of the BDA had come to the suit property on April 24, 2001 and demolished the existing structure. This act of the BDA would amply demonstrate that there was no unhindered, peaceful and continuous possession of the suit land.[22]

2.Learned Counsel for the Respondent had raised the plea of equity. He has also submitted that when the BDA itself is created for the purpose of formation of layouts and allotment of sites to the members of the public, the Respondent should not be dispossessed when she is in continuous possession of the suit property. However, these would not be the relevant considerations in the present case as the Court cannot forget that the present appeal arises out of civil proceedings filed in the form of a suit by the Respondent and once it is found that the Respondent has not been able to prove title by adverse possession, no such aspects, not coming within the scope of the suit proceedings, can be looked into.[23]

3. Insofar as the argument predicated on Section 27 of the Bangalore Development Authority Act or Section 24(2) of the Right to Fair Compensation and Transparency in Land Acquisition Rehabilitation and Resettlement Act, 2013 are concerned, again these issues were neither raised nor arise in the instant case. If the Respondent, if at all, has any right to make claim on the aforesaid grounds, in any appropriate proceedings, she can do so, if permissible in law. The Court clarified that it has not gone into these issues and, therefore, has not made any comments on the merits of such pleas raised by the Respondent.[23]

4. As a result, the appeal stands allowed resulting in dismissal of the suit filed by the Respondent in the trial court.[24]

CHAPTER SIXTEEN

M. Venkatesh and Ors. vs. Commissioner, Bangalore Development Authority and Ors. (24.09.2015 - SC) : MANU/SC/1081/2015

Relative Section:

Land Acquisition Act Section 16(2)

Hon'bleJudges/Coram:

T.S. Thakur, R.K. Agrawal and R. Banumathi

Equivalent Citation:

Case Reference:

John B. James and Ors. v. Bangalore Development Authority MANU/KA/0046/2001 : (2001) 1 Kar LJ 364;

U.P. Jal Nigam v. Kalra Properties Pvt. Ltd. MANU/SC/0310/1996 : AIR 1996 SC 1170;

Ajay Kishan Singhal v. Union of India MANU/SC/0675/1996 : AIR 1996 SC 2677;

Mahavir and Anr. v. Rural Institute, Amravati and Anr. MANU/SC/0763/1995 : (1995) 5 SCC 335;

Gian Chand v. Gopala and Ors. (1995) 5 SCC 528;

Meera Sahni v. Lieutenant Governor of Delhi and Ors. MANU/SC/7878/2008 : (2008) 9 SCC 177;

Tika Ram v. State of U.P. MANU/SC/1616/2009 : (2009) 10 SCC 689;

Tamil Nadu Housing Board v. A. Viswam (dead) by L.Rs. MANU/SC/
0924/1996 : AIR 1996 SC 3377;

Larsen and Toubro Ltd. v. State of Gujarat and Ors. MANU/SC/0219/
1998 : AIR 1998 SC 1608;

Karnataka Board of Wakf v. Govt. of India MANU/SC/0377/2004 :
(2004) 10 SCC 779; S.M. Karim v. Bibi Sakina (MANU/SC/0236/1964 : AIR
1964 SC 1254;

Parsinni v. Sukhi MANU/SC/0575/1993 : (1993) 4 SCC 375;

D.N. Venkatarayappa v. State of Karnataka MANU/SC/0766/1997 :
(1997) 7 SCC 567; Mahesh Chand Sharma (Dr.) v. Raj Kumari Sharma
MANU/SC/0231/1996 : (1996) 8 SCC 128;

Saroop Singh v. Banto MANU/SC/1146/2005 : (2005) 8 SCC 330;

Vasantiben Prahladji Nayak v. Somnath Muljibhai Nayak MANU/SC/
0216/2004 : (2004) 3 SCC 376;

Mohd. Mohd. Ali v. Jagadish Kalita (2004) 1 SCC 371;

Mohan Lal v. Mirza Abdul Gaffar MANU/SC/1039/1996 : (1996) 1 SCC
639;

Annasaheb Bapusaheb Patil v. Balwant MANU/SC/0172/1995 : (1995)
2 SCC 543

M. Venkatesh and Ors. vs. Commissioner, Bangalore Development
Authority and Ors. (24.09.2015 - SC) : MANU / SC/ 1081/2015

NumberofPagesintheOriginalJudgment:

Case Note:

Land Acquisition - Ownership claim over suit property - Appellant-
M Venkatesh and Prabhaudas Patel - Claimed ownership by inheritance -
Respective suit property - Said parcels of land acquired by BDA - Suits
filed by aggrieved parties - Prayer - Order restraining BDA from interfering
- Peaceful occupation - Trial Court decreed suit - Favour of plaintiffs -
RFAs filed by BDA - Single Judge allowed all but one - RFA No. 911 of
2002 - High Court upheld Trial Court's judgment and decree - High Court
judgment assailed - SLP - Whether the Appellants prove their alleged lawful
possession and enjoyment of suit scheduled properties - Whether
Prabhaudas Patel and otherRespondents in SLP (C) No. 12016 of 2013 were
entitled to any relief from the Court - Whether the Appellants prove that,
they have acquired and perfected their alleged title to the suit schedule
properties by virtue of the alleged law on adverse possession

Facts:

M. Venkatesh-Appellant in SLP (C) No. 38601 of 2012 claimed ownership over the suit schedule property by inheritance from his grandfather who had purchased the same under a registered sale-deed. In connected SLP (C) No. 12016 of 2013 Prabhaudas Patel also claimed to be the owner of suit schedule property relevant to his suit on the basis of purchase of said property from its previous owner. The aforementioned two parcels of land together with a larger extent in the vicinity were acquired by the Bangalore Development Authority (BDA) for the formation of Hosur Road, Sarjapur Layout.

BDA claimed that possession of the land was taken over from the landowners and handed over to the engineering section of the authority by drawing a possession mahazar. A Notification Under Section 16(2) of the Act was also published in the Karnataka Gazette dated 4th July, 1991 which, as per BDA, signified that the land in question stood vested with the BDA free from all encumbrances whatsoever. BDA alleges that long after the land had vested in the BDA, sites were carved out and sold to different persons by the erstwhile owners, the unauthorised act of the Plaintiffs, however, got vacated and the possession was taken over.

The case of the Plaintiffs M. Venkatesh and Prabhaudas Patel on the other hand was that they were always in established possession of the suit schedule property and that apprehending their dispossession from the same they had approached the High Court along with several others to restrain BDA from interfering with their peaceful occupation of suit property. High Court disposed of petitions reserving liberty to approach the civil court for appropriate relief and hence, number of originial suits came to be filed by the aggrieved parties in which the Plaintiffs claimed to be the owners and occupants of the suit property and prayed for an order restraining the BDA from interfering with their peaceful occupation.

Trial Court decreed the suits in favour of plaintiffs. Aggrieved by the judgment and decree of Trial Court, BDA filed RFA Nos. 911, 912,914, 915 and 916 of 2002 before High Court. A single judge allowed all but dismissed RFA No.911 of 2002 taking the view that Respondents were running a saw-mill which was in operation long prior to the filing of the suit and which continues to be in existence even on the date of the suit and the judgment of the High Court. BDA upheld the judgment and decree passed by the Trial Court restraining BDA from interfering with possession. As regards the remaining appeals, High Court held that the Plaintiffs threin were claiming settled possession of vacant pieces of land which did not entitle them to any relief as no one could claim to be in established possession of a vacant piece of land.

In SLP (C) No. 12016 of 2013 the BDA has assailed the judgment of the High Court dismissing RFA No. 911 of 2002 whereas SLP (C) No. 38601 of 2012 and SLP (C) Nos. 12013-15 of 2013 have been filed by Appellants to assail High Court's order.

Held by Hon'ble Supreme Court

(I) There is, in our opinion, no infirmity in High Court's reasoning. The decision in John B. James and Ors. v. Bangalore Development Authority upon which heavy reliance was placed by the Plaintiffs before the courts below itself did not permit anyone to claim that he is in settled possession of vacant land.[11]

(II) Once the High Court recorded a finding that the property was vacant as on the date of the filing of the suit there was no question of the Plaintiffs claiming settled possession of the said property assuming the view taken in John B. James and Ors. v. Bangalore Development Authority was otherwise legally sound since the so called settled possession of the Appellants in RFA No. 911 of 2002 stood vacated from the suit schedule property, no prayer for injunction as set out in the petition filed by the Appellants in those appeals could help them for an injunction issues only to protect what is in lawful possession of the Plaintiffs. Injunction could not be claimed when Plaintiffs stand dispossessed from the suit property prior to the filing of the suit. The question of establishing settled possession did not, therefore, arise in relation to the properties that already stood cleared of any structures by demolition of whatever stood on the same. The High Court was, in that view, justified in setting aside the decree passed by the Trial Court and dismissing the suit filed by the Plaintiffs.[12]

(III) That brings us to the question whether Prabhaudas Patel and other Respondents in SLP (C) No. 12016 of 2013 were entitled to any relief from the Court. These Respondents claim to have purchased the suit property in terms of a sale deed dated 22nd August, 1990, i.e. long after the issue of the preliminary notification published in July 1984. The legal position about the validity of any such sale, post issue of a preliminary notification is fairly well settled by a long line of the decisions of this Court. The sale in such cases is void and non-est in the eyes of law giving to the Vendee the limited right to claim compensation and no more.[13]

(IV) More importantly, as on the date of the suit, the Respondents had not completed 12 years in possession of the suit property so as to entitle them to claim adverse possession against BDA, the true owner. The argument that possession of the land was never taken also needs notice only to be rejected for it is settled that one of the modes of taking possession is by drawing a Panchnama which part has been done to perfection according to the evidence led by the Defendant-BDA.[14]

(V) Coming then to the question whether the Plaintiffs- Respondents could claim adverse possession, we need to hardly mention the well known and oft-quoted maxim nec vi, nec clam, nec precario meaning thereby that adverse possession is proved only when possession is peaceful, open, continuous and hostile.[15]

(VI) Also noteworthy is the decision of this Court in Mohan Lal v. Mirza Abdul Gaffar, where this Court held that claim of title to the property and adverse possession are in terms contradictory. The Courts below have not seen the Plaintiff - Respondent's claim from the above perspectives. The High Court has, in particular, remained oblivious of the principle enunciated in the decisions to which we have referred herein above. All that the High Court has found in favour of the Plaintiffs is that their possession is established. That, however, does not conclude the controversy.[19]

(VII) The question is not just whether the Plaintiffs were in possession, but whether they had by being in adverse possession for the statutory period of 12 years perfected their title. That question has neither been adverted to nor answered in the judgment impugned in this appeal. Such being the case the High Court, in our opinion, erred in dismissing the appeal filed by the Appellant-BDA. The fact that the Plaintiffs had not and could not possibly establish their adverse possession over the suit property should have resulted in dismissal of the suit for an unauthorised occupant had no right to claim relief that would perpetuate his illegal and unauthorised occupation of property that stood vested in the BDA.[19]

CHAPTER SEVENTEEN

Ram Nagina Rai and Ors. vs. Deo Kumar Rai and Ors. (21.08.2018 - SC) : MANU/SC/1003/2018

Relative Section:

Limitation Act, 1963 - Schedule - Article 64, Limitation Act, 1963 - Schedule - Article 65

Hon'bleJudges/Coram:

N.V. Ramana and Mohan M. Shantanagoudar

Equivalent Citation: 2018(II)CLR(SC)921, 2019(1)J.L.J.R.338, 2019(1)PLJR371, 2018(10)SCALE630, (2019)13SCC324, 2018 (10) SCJ 533

Case Reference:

P.T. Munichikkanna Reddy and Ors. v. Revamma and Ors. MANU/SC/7325/2007 : (2007) 6 SCC 59;

Thakur Kishan Singh v. Arvind Kumar MANU/SC/0015/1995 : (1994) 6 SCC 591; Powell v. McFarlane (1977) 38 P & CR (Property, Planning and Compensation Reports) 452;

Hemaji Waghaji v. Bhikhabhai Khengarbhai and Ors. MANU/SC/4083/2008 : (2009) 16 SCC 517;

State of Haryana v. Mukesh Kumar MANU/SC/1147/2011 : (2011) 10 SCC 404

NumberofPagesintheOriginalJudgment:6

Case Note:

Property - Title - Declaration - Present appeal filed to challenge judgment and decree passed by lower Appellate Court in suit filed for seeking declaration of title in suit property - Whether impugned judgment and decree under challenge needs interference - Held, no absolute requirement to deem mere possession of suit property by Defendants to amount to adverse possession - Nothing on record to show that Defendants' permissive possession over property became adverse to interest of possession - Impugned judgment and decree set aside - Appeal allowed. [14] real owner - Records reveal that permissive possession of Defendants continued till filing of suit - Courts below erred in concluding that Defendants perfected their title by adverse

Facts:

1. This appeal is directed against the judgment and order dated 17.10.2003, passed by the learned Single Judge of the High Court of Judicature at Patna in Second Appeal No. 403 of 1998. By the impugned judgment, the High Court confirmed the judgment and decree dated 30.06.1998 passed by the 9th Additional District Judge, Bhojpurat Arrah in Title Appeal No. 26/97. The records reveal that the Appellants being the Plaintiffs in Title Suit No. 64/89 in the court of Munsif III, Arrah (Bhojpur) filed a suit for declaration of title and recovery of possession in respect of the suit house situated over new Plot No. 2909 under new Khata No. 699, area measuring 10 decimals. The suit came to be decreed by the Trial Court in favour of the Plaintiffs. The contesting Defendants filed Title Appeal No. 26/97 9th before the Additional District Judge, Bhojpur at Arrah, which came to be allowed, setting aside the judgment of the Trial Court; consequently, the suit of the Appellants herein was dismissed. The judgment of the District Court, i.e. the First Appellate Court, dated 30.06.1998 was confirmed by the High Court in second appeal on 17.10.2003. Thus, the unsuccessful Plaintiffs are before us questioning the judgment of the High Court as well as the First Appellate Court.

2. The case of the Plaintiffs is that the disputed house was in their ownership and the khata of the property was recorded in the name of their ancestor. Since the Defendants' ancestor was on friendly terms with the plaintiffs' ancestor, and as Plaintiffs' ancestor was in a different place for business, the Defendants were permitted to occupy the disputed house. The Defendants got khatian changed without notice to the Plaintiffs, showing the Defendants to be in possession of the disputed house. Since the Defendants did not hand over possession of the property to the Plaintiffs,

despite many requests by the Plaintiffs, the suit came to be filed.

The case of the contesting Defendants is that they are the owners in possession of the suit house even prior to 1953. Their ancestor, viz. Sheomuni Rai, had friendly relations with the Plaintiffs' grandfather, Pitambar Rai. At the time of the revision survey, the concerned authorities having found that the Defendants are in possession of the property, R.S. Khatian was prepared in their names. R.S. Khatian was finally published in the year 1970, but the Plaintiff filed the Title Suit only 19 years after its final publication and hence, the suit is barred by limitation. It is further the case of the Defendants that they have become owners of the property by virtue of their adverse possession over the suit property. In other words, the Defendants contended that they had perfected the title by adverse possession and therefore the Plaintiffs are not entitled to recover the possession of the suit house from the Defendants.

3. The only question to be decided in this appeal is, whether the First Appellate Court and the High Court were justified in concluding that the Defendants have perfected the title by adverse possession over the suit property. Heard the arguments on both the sides, and perused the records at hand.

4. At the outset, it is relevant to mention that the Defendants have not produced any document to show that they are the owners of the suit property by purchasing the same or by acquiring the same by any mode of transfer. Also, there is nothing on record to show that the property in question is the ancestral property of the Defendants. However, alternative case of the Defendants that the Plaintiffs were the owners of the property and had permitted the Defendants' ancestor and thereafter, the Defendants to be in possession of the property. In other words, the Defendants do admit that the Plaintiffs are the owners of the property. But the sole contention of the contesting Defendants is that they have perfected the title by adverse possession, and that the suit to claim possession of the suit property is beyond the period of limitation. The Plaintiffs do admit that the Defendants are in permissive possession of the property, but claim that khatian changed in the name of Defendants was without notice to the Plaintiffs and the same cannot be relied upon. It is the specific case of the Plaintiffs that the Defendants have not perfected the title by virtue of adverse possession.

5. Since the contesting Defendants have raised a plea of adverse possession, the burden is on them to prove affirmatively that the bar of limitation prescribed Under Article 65 of the Schedule of the Limitation

Act, 1963, viz., 12 years, is applicable in the matter to file a suit for possession of immovable property based on title. The limitation of 12 years begins when the possession of the Defendants would become adverse to that of the Plaintiffs. Thus, it is incumbent on the Plaintiffs to file a suit for possession within 12 years from when the possession of the Defendants becomes adverse to. the Plaintiffs. Article 65 presupposes that the limitation starts only if the Defendants prove the factum of adverse possession affirmatively from a particular time. Adverse possession means a hostile assertion, i.e. a possession which is expressly or impliedly in denial of the title of the true owner. The person who bases his title on adverse possession must show, by clear and unequivocal evidence, that the possession was hostile to the real owner and it amounted to the denial of his title to the property claimed. In deciding whether the acts alleged by the person constitute adverse possession, regard must be given to the animus of the person doing such acts, which must be ascertained from the facts and circumstances of each case. It is needless to observe that where the possession can be referred to a lawful title, it would not be considered to be adverse, the reason being that the person whose possession can be drawn to a lawful title, will not be permitted to show that his possession was hostile to another's title. Simply put, one who holds possession on behalf of another, does not by mere denial of the other's title, make his possession adverse so as to give himself the benefit of the statute of limitation.

6. In the matter on hand, though the Defendants have pleaded that they are the owners of the property, it seems that during the course of the trial, they have given up this contention, inasmuch as they have only concentrated on the contention that they have perfected the title by adverse possession. All through, as is evident from the material evidence on record and their contentions, the Defendants have tried to show that they have been in continuous possession of the property for more than 60 years. But there is no iota of evidence to show as to when the Defendants' possession in fact became adverse to the interest of the Plaintiff. Except for the change of khatian sometime in the year 1970 by the Defendants and the payment of taxes for being in possession of property, no material is produced by the Defendants to show whether the possession was really hostile to the actual owner. There is absolutely nothing on record to show that there was a hostile assertion by the Defendants. We do not find that the Defendants had hostile animus at any point of time, from the facts and circumstances of this case. The Defendants denied the title of the Plaintiffs over the suit property

only when the suit came to be filed, inasmuch as the Defendants have taken such a contention for the first time in their written statements.

7. The non-use of the property by the owner even for a long time may affect the title of the owner under certain circumstances. The acquisition of title by adverse possession springs into action essentially by default or inaction of the owner. There is a lot of difference between simple possession and adverse possession. Every possession is not adverse possession. The Defendants will not acquire adverse possession by simply remaining in permissive possession for howsoever long it may be.

8. Until the Defendants' possession becomes adverse to that of the real owner, the Defendants continue in permissive possession of the property. Only if the Defendants' possession becomes adverse to the interest of the real owner and the real owner fails to file the suit for possession within 12 years, as prescribed Under Article 65 of the Limitation Act, from the point of time the possession by the Defendants becomes adverse to the Plaintiffs, the real owner loses his title over the property.

Held by Hon'ble Supreme Court

The Defendants are not only required to prove that they have been in possession of the suit property continuously and uninterruptedly, but also need to prove, by cogent and convincing evidence, that there is hostile animus and possession adverse to the knowledge of the real owner.

This Court, while discussing the law relating to adverse possession in P.T. Munichikkanna Reddy and Ors. v. Revamma and Ors. MANU/SC/ 7325/2007 : (2007) 6 SCC 59 p. 68 P. 8, held that, to assess a claim of adverse possession, a two-pronged enquiry is required; viz. application of the limitation provisions, and the specific positive intention to dispossess on the part of the adverse possessor.

This aforementioned observation was reiterated by this Court in a subsequent judgment of State of Haryana v. Mukesh Kumar MANU/SC/ 1147/2011 : (2011) 10 SCC 404 wherein the Court observed that the law of adverse possession needs a re-look, holding the right to property to be a human right, in addition to it being a constitutional or a statutory right.

1. In light of the above observations of this Court, we find that there is no absolute requirement to deem the mere possession of the suit property by the Defendants to amount to adverse possession over the suit property. This would be in clear violation of the basic rights of the actual owner of the property. There is nothing on record to show that the Defendants' permissive possession over the property became adverse to the interest of

the real owner, at any point of time. On the contrary, the records reveal that the permissive possession of the Defendants continued till the filing of the suit.

2. The Defendants have relied upon certain paid tax receipts and khatian extracts. The Trial Court has, on facts, specifically found that these documents do not disclose the khatian and plot number, and even the tax receipts do not relate to the suit house. Also, the chaukidari receipts (A 1 to A16) do not contain the khatian of the suit house. These receipts have been unfortunately believed to prove that the Defendants are in adverse possession of- the-disputed land. Even assuming that those documents relate to" the suit house, they, at the most, depict the possession of the Defendants and not their, adverse possession.

3. Having regard to the totality of the facts, in our considered opinion/ the First Appellate Court as well as the High Court are not justified in arriving at the conclusion that the contesting Defendants have perfected their title by adverse possession. In view of the same, the judgment of the High Court as also the judgment of The 9th Additional District Judge, Bhojpur at Arrah are set aside. The judgments of the Trial Court i.e. the Court of Munsif III, Arrah (Bhojpur) in Title Suit No. 64/89 is restored. Appeal is allowed accordingly.

CHAPTER EIGHTEEN

Mallikarjunaiah vs. Nanjaiah and Ors. (26.04.2019 – SC) : MANU/SC/0607/2019

Relative Section:

Civil Appeal

Hon'bleJudges/Coram:

Abhay Manohar Sapre and Dinesh Maheshwari

Equivalent Citation:

Case Reference:

T. Anjanappa and Ors. v. Somalingappa and Anr. MANU/SC/8429/2006 : (2006) 7 SCC 570;

Chatti Konati Rao and Ors. v. Palle Venkata Subba Rao MANU/SC/1033/2010

NumberofPagesintheOriginalJudgment:

Case Note:

Property - Possession - Present appeal is directed against the final judgment passed by High Court whereby the High Court partly allowed appeal filed by Appellant and declared Appellant (Plaintiff) to be owner in respect of land admeasuring 19 Guntas in and 11 Guntas but dismissed his claim as being the owner of the suit land admeasuring 1 Gunta and instead declared the Defendants to be its owner by virtue of their adverse possession over the suit land - Whether High Court was justified in holding that, Defendants (Respondents) had become owner of suit land to extent of 1 Gunta by virtue of their adverse possession over it.

Facts:

Appellant filed a civil suit in the year 1992 against the Respondents for declaration of his ownership right over the entire land including the suit land and for grant of permanent injunction in relation to the suit land. In the alternative, the Appellant also sought the relief of possession of the suit land in case, he is held to be not in possession of the suit land. The Trial Court, while partly decreeing the suit, by judgment declared the Appellant (Plaintiff) as the owner of larger part of Schedule 'A' property but observed that the Defendants had perfected their title by adverse possession over 1 Gunta of land in Sy. No. 17/3 and, therefore, the prayer seeking permanent injunction against the Defendants as regards Schedule 'B' property was rejected. The Appellant (Plaintiff) felt aggrieved and filed first appeal before the first Appellate Court. By order, the first Appellate Court, in substance, upheld all the findings of the trial Court but modified the decree to some extent regarding the measurement of the suit land. The Appellant (Plaintiff) felt aggrieved and filed second appeal in the High Court of Karnataka. By impugned judgment, the High Court partly allowed the appeal and declared the Appellant (Plaintiff) to be the owner in respect of the land admeasuring 19Guntas in Sy. No. 17/3 and 11 Guntas in Sy. No. 34/ 3 but dismissed his claim as being the owner of the suit land admeasuring 1 Gunta in Sy. No. 17/3 and instead declared the Defendants to be its owner by virtue of their adverse possession over the suit land.

Held, while allowing the appeal

1. The Courts below were not justified in holding that, the Defendants have perfected their title over the suit land qua the Plaintiff by virtue of their adverse possession over the suit land. [21]

2. Appellant (Plaintiff) was the owner of the entire land including the suit land, i.e., encroached portion, which was alleged to be in possession of the Respondents (Defendants). In other words, the Respondents (Defendants) have admitted the ownership of the Appellant (Plaintiff) over the entire land including the suit land by setting up the plea of adverse possession over it. Burden to prove the adverse possession was on the Respondents (Defendants) because it was they who had set up this plea. Respondents (Defendants) failed to discharge this burden. There was no element of either adversity or/and hostility between two co-owners/ brothers because in a dispute of this nature where both the parties are related to each other, the possession of one is regarded to be the possession of other unless the facts show otherwise. Respondents (Defendants) failed to adduce any evidence to prove that they were asserting their right of

ownership over the entire land or the suit land or its part openly and to the knowledge of the Appellant (Plaintiff) continuously for a period of more than 12 years. It is a settled principle of law that mere continuous possession howsoever long it may have been qua its true owner is not enough to sustain the plea of adverse possession unless it is further proved that such possession was open, hostile, exclusive and with the assertion of ownership right over the property to the knowledge of its true owner. Such is not the case here. Present was a case where both the parties were not aware as to how much land was in exclusive possession of each. Here is a case where both the parties to the suit did not know as to how much land was in the exclusive possession of the Appellant (Plaintiff) and how much land was in possession of the Respondents (Defendants). It was only when the Appellant (Plaintiff) got the suit land measured through the revenue department in the year 1983, he came to know that some portion of the land, which had fallen to his share was in possession of the Respondents (Defendants). [22]

3. Thereafter the Appellant (Plaintiff) filed a suit in the year 1992 against the Respondents (Defendants) for declaration and injunction and in the alternative also claimed possession of the suit land. The suit was, therefore, filed well within the period of 12 years from the date of knowledge, i.e., in the year 1983. During this period also, there was no evidence adduced by the Defendants to prove that they ever asserted their right of ownership over the specific portion of the suit land as belonging to them openly and with assertion of hostility to the knowledge of Appellant (Plaintiff). [23]

4. The Appellant (Plaintiff) having come to know that the Respondents (Defendants) had encroached upon his land in the year 1983 and he rightly filed the suit within 12 years from the date of knowledge, a plea of adverse possession was not available to the Respondents (Defendants) against the Appellant (Plaintiff) because 12 years had not been completed by then. [24]

5. The question of Respondents (Defendants) perfecting their title by adverse possession over the suit land did not arise. Even if the Respondents (Defendants) claimed to be in possession over the suit land prior to the year 1983, the same was of no consequence for the simple reason that such possession was neither exclusive nor hostile and nor it was to the knowledge of the parties for want of actual measurements. [25]

6. The Courts below were not justified in declaring the Respondents (Defendants) to be the owner of the encroached portion of the suit land by

virtue of adverse possession. This finding being against the settled principle of law deserves to be set aside. [26]

7. Appeal allowed. The impugned judgment is set aside. As a consequence thereof, the Plaintiff's (Appellant's) suit is decreed in its entirety against the Defendants. The Defendants (Respondents) are granted three months' time to vacate the encroached portion (1 Gunta in Sy. No. 17/3) and hand over its possession to the Appellant/Plaintiff. [27]

State of Haryana vs. Mukesh Kumar and Ors. (30.09.2011 - SC) : MANU/SC/1147/2011

Relative Section:

Constitution Of India - Article 1, Article 41

Hon'bleJudges/Coram:

Dalveer Bhandari and Deepak Verma

Equivalent Citation: AIR2012SC559, 2012(2)ALD101(SC), 2012 (90) ALR 216, 2012(1)ALT1(SC), 2011(3)ARC655, 2012 1 AWC997SC, 2012(3)CHN168, 2012(1)CLJ(SC)129, 2011(II)CLR(SC)905, 2011GLH(3)592, 2011 (4) KLT(SN) 63, 2011-5-LW725, 2012(1)RCR(Civil)17, RLW2012(2)SC1280, 2011(11)SCALE266, (2011)10SCC404, 2011(6)UJ4099

Case Reference:

S.M. Karim v. Mst. Bibi Sakina MANU/SC/0236/1964 : AIR 1964 SC 1254;

Bhim Singh and Ors. v. Zile Singh and Ors. MANU/PH/0354/2006 : AIR 2006 P&H 195;

Food Corporation of India and Anr. v. Dayal Singh 1991 PLJ 425;

Kanak Ram and Ors. v. Chanan Singh and Ors. MANU/PH/0125/2007 : (2007) 146 PLR 498;

Hemaji Waghaji Jat v. Bhikhabhai Khengarbhai Harijan and Ors. MANU/SC/4083/2008 : (2009)16 SCC 517;

Downing v. Bird 100 So 2d 57 (Fla 1958); Arkansas Commemorative Commission v. City of Little Rock 227 Ark 1085 : 303 SW 2d 569 (1957);

Monnot v. Murphy 207 NY 240 : 100 NE 742 (1913); City of Rock Springs v. Sturm 39 Wyo 494 ; 273 P 908 ; (1929) 97 ALR 1;

Fairweather v. St Marylebone Property Co (1962) 2 WLR 1020 : (1962) 2 All ER 288;

Taylor v. Twinberrow (1930) 2 K.B. 16;

Beaulane Properties Ltd. v. Palmer (2005) 3 WLR 554;

JA Pye (Oxford) Ltd. v. United Kingdom (2005) 49 ERG 90;

JA Pye (Oxford) Ltd. v. Graham (2003) 1 AC 419 : (2002) 3 WLR 221 ;

(2002) 3 All ER 865 (HL) ;

(2000) 3 WLR 242 ; 2000 Ch 676;

P.T. Munichikkanna Reddy v. Revamma MANU/SC/7325/2007 : (2007) 6 SCC 59;

Beyeler v. Italy (GC) No. 33202 of 1996

NumberofPagesintheOriginalJudgment: 11

Case Note:

Property - Adverse possession - Whether the State, which is in charge of protection of life, liberty and property of the people could be permitted to grab the land and property of its own citizens under the banner of the plea of adverse possession?

Facts:

1. People are often astonished to learn that a trespasser may take the title of a building or land from the true owner in certain conditions and such theft is even authorized by law.

2. The theory of adverse possession is also perceived by the general public as a dishonest way to obtain title to property. Property right advocates argue that mistakes by landowners or negligence on their part should never transfer their property rights to a wrongdoer, who never paid valuable consideration for such an interest.

3. The government itself may acquire land by adverse possession. Fairness dictates and commands that if the government can acquire title to private land through adverse possession, it should be able to lose title under the same circumstances.

4. We have heard the Learned Counsel for the State of Haryana. We do not deem it appropriate to financially burden the Respondents by issuing notice in this Special Leave Petition. A very vital question which arises for consideration in this petition is whether the State, which is in charge of protection of life, liberty and property of the people can be permitted to grab the land and property of its own citizens under the banner of the plea

of adverse possession?

5. Brief facts, relevant to dispose of this Special Leave Petition are recapitulated as under:

6. The State of Haryana had filed a Civil Suit through the Superintendent of Police, Gurgaon, seeking a relief of declaration to the effect that it has acquired the rights of ownership by way of adverse possession over land measuring 8 biswas comprising khewat No. 34, khata No. 56, khasra No. 3673/452 situated in the revenue estate of Hidayatpur Chhavni, Haryana.

7. The other prayer in the suit was that the sale deed dated 26th March, 1990, mutation No. 3690 dated 22nd November, 1990 as well as judgment and decree dated 19th May, 1992, passed in Civil Suit No. 368 dated 9th March, 1991 are liable to be set aside. As a consequential relief, it was also prayed that the Defendants be perpetually restrained from interfering with the peaceful possession of the Plaintiff (petitioner herein) over the suit land. For the sake of convenience we are referring the Petitioner as the Plaintiff and the Respondents as Defendants.

8. In the written statement, the Defendants raised a number of preliminary objections pertaining to estoppel, cause of action and mis-joinder of necessary parties. It was specifically denied that the Plaintiff ever remained in possession of the suit property for the last 55 years. It was submitted that the disputed property was still lying vacant. However, the Plaintiff recently occupied it by using force and thereafter have also raised a boundary wall of police line. It was denied in the written statement that the Plaintiff acquired right of ownership by way of adverse possession qua property in question. The Defendants prayed for dismissal of suit and by way of a counter claim also prayed for a decree for possession qua suit property be passed.

Held, while allowing the appeal

Held, Article 1 of Protocol 1 to Convention for Protection of Human Rights and Fundamental Freedoms provided that every natural or legal person was entitled to peaceful enjoyment of his possession and no one should be deprived of his possession except in public interest. It was cleared from revenue records of State that disputed property stood in name of Defendants . However, Superintendent of Police, senior official of Indian Police Service made repeated attempted to grab property of true owner by filing repeated appeals before different forums claiming right of ownership by way of adverse possession. Though, Government should protect property of citizen and not steal it and if protectors of law become grabbers of property, then people would be left with no protection and there would be total anarchy in entire country. Therefore, it cleared that no Government Department, Public Undertaking and much less Police Department should be permitted to perfect title of land or building by invoking provisions of adverse possession and grab property of its own citizens. Petition dismissed.

Ratio Decidendi:

"No Government Department, Public Undertaking, and much less the Police Department should be permitted to perfect the title of the land or building by invoking the provisions of adverse possession and grab the property of its own citizens."

Bapusaheb Chimasaheb Naik-Nimbalkar (Dead through L.Rs.) and Ors. vs. Mahesh Vijaysinha Rajebhosale and Ors. (25.04.2017 - SC) : MANU/SC/0516/201

Relative Section:
　　Hindu Succession Act, 1956 - Section 14(1),
　　Hindu Succession Act, 1956 - Section 14(2);
　　Code of Civil Procedure, 1908 (CPC) - Order II Rule 2;
　　Limitation Act, 1963 - Schedule - Article 65,
　　Limitation Act, 1963 - Schedule - Article 141
Hon'bleJudges/Coram:
Arun Mishra and S. Abdul Nazeer

Equivalent Citation: 2017(4)ABR628, 2017(176)AIC154, AIR2017SC2491, 2017(4)ALD163, 2017 (123) ALR 791, 2017(3)BLJ82, 2017(4)BomCR31, (2018)1CALLT1(SC), 2017 (3) CCC 19 , 2017(3)CDR549(SC), 2017(3) CHN (SC) 91, 124(2017)CLT244, 2017(I)CLR(SC)1192, 2017/INSC/393, 2017(3)J.L.J.R.72, 2017-4-LW958, 2018(1)MhLj11, 2018(1)MPLJ1, 2017(3)PLJR163, 2017(3)RCR(Civil)183,

2017 137 RD253, 2017(5)SCALE363, (2017)7SCC769, 2017 (5) SCJ 201, [2017]3SCR387, (2017)6WBLR(SC)156, 2018 (1) WLN 137 (SC)

Case Reference:

Hashmat Begam and Anr. v. Mazhar Husain and Ors. MANU/UP/0013/1888 : (1888) ILR 10 All. 343;

Ghisa Singh and Anr. v. Gajraj Singh AIR 1916 Oudh 50;

Mohammad Yaqub v. Bijai Lal AIR 1918 Oudh 32;

Zarif un-nisa and Ors. v. Chaudhri Shafiq-uz-zaman and Ors. AIR 1923 Oudh 185;

Malkarjun Mahadev Belure v. Amrita Tukaram Dambare andOrs.MANU/MH/0057/1918 : AIR1918 Bom. 142;

Jagat Ram v. Varinder Prakash MANU/SC/8044/2006 : (2006) 4 SCC 482;

Ranbir Singh and Ors. v. Kartar Singh and Ors. MANU/SC/0164/2003 : AIR 2003 SC 1858;

Amar Singh and Ors. v. Sewa Ram and Ors. MANU/PH/0271/1960 : AIR 1960 Punjab 530;

Harak Singh v. Kailash Singh and Anr. MANU/BH/0191/1958 : AIR 1958 Pat. 581;

Mt. Lukai W/o Katikram and Ors. v. Niranjan Dayaram and Ors. MANU/MP/0056/1958 : AIR 1958 MP 160; State of M.P. v. State of Maharashtra MANU/SC/0241/1977 : (1977) 2 SCC 288;

State of Maharashtra v. National Construction Co. MANU/SC/0597/1996 : (1996) 1 SCC 735;

Bengal Waterproof Ltd. v. Bombay Waterproof Mfg. Co. MANU/SC/0327/1997 : (1997) 1 SCC 99;

Deva Ram v. Ishwar Chand MANU/SC/0097/1996 : (1995) 6 SCC 733;

Gurbux Singh v. Bhooralal MANU/SC/0241/1964 : AIR 1964 SC 1810

NumberofPagesintheOriginalJudgment:9

Case Note:

Property - Suit for partition - Maintainability thereof - Order II Rule 2 of Code of Civil Procedure, 1908 - Plaintiffs/Respondents filed suit for partition of land against Defendants/Appellants - Trial Court decreed suit - Held Plaintiffs and Defendants to be co-owners and in joint possession of suit land on date of suit - Defendants were not in exclusive possession - No ouster of Plaintiff - Suit for partition was not barred by limitation - Nor it was barred by provisions of Order II Rule 2 of Code, 1908 - Appellate Court had also affirmed findings - High Court dismissed second appeal

- Hence, present appeal - Whether judgment and decree passed by Trial Court affirmed by District Court and High Court were sustainable

Facts:

The Plaintiffs/Respondents, sons and daughters of the deceased, filed a suit for partition of the land. The Plaintiffs averred that the land was ancestral property initially inherited by a person who had three wives. That person had a son who had a daughter, who died issueless. The deceased/ sister of person's son succeeded to the property. She also died and her property was inherited by the Plaintiffs being her sons and daughters. The suit was filed against another son of person in question. Appellant Nos. 1 and 2 were successors of the another son.

The Trial Court decreed the suit and held the Plaintiffs and Defendants to be co-owners and in joint possession of the suit land on the date of the suit. The Defendants were not in exclusive possession. The right, title and interest of the deceased was not denied by the another son. There was no ouster of the Plaintiff. The suit for partition could not be said to be barred by limitation. Nor it was barred by provisions of Order II Rule 2 of Code of Civil Procedure, 1908. The Appellate Court had also affirmed the findings. The second appeal preferred had also been dismissed. Hence, the present appeal.

Held, while dismissing the appeal:

(i) It is necessary to trace the right to someone else and not to the Hindu or Mohammedan female, as the case may be. The daughter of first son became absolute owner of the property on 6.2.1958 and on her death on 1.10.1962, the right accrued to the deceased on the basis of inheritance made from her who was the owner of the 1/2 share in question. When the property is claimed from a woman, Hindu or Mohammedan, who was the full owner, it could not be said that the deceased or the Plaintiffs became entitled to the property independently of the rights of female i.e. The daughter. Thus the suit filed by such heir of female for separate possession/ partition would not be governed by Explanation (b) to Article 65. In such a case limitation would not commence as per Explanation (b) to Article 65 on death of female Hindu. However, the starting point of limitation for computation of 12 years would be the date of start of adverse possession otherwise. The daughter of first son was not having life-interest but she was the full owner of the property, thus Article 65(b) of the Limitation Act, 1963 had no application. [8] and[10]

(ii) Possession never became adverse to the Plaintiffs. There was concurrent finding recorded that the Plaintiffs were in joint possession of the disputed land on the date of filing of the suit. The Defendants had taken the plea of ouster and the suit was filed beyond 12 years of death of the daughter but they were not able to prove their adverse possession. As adverse possession was not concurrently found by the three courts and in this case the starting point of limitation would not be the date of death of the daughter in the year 1962 as she was full owner, as such suit could not be said to be barred by limitation. [13]

(iii) The cause of action of the suit for partition was different and dispute as to mutation had been subsequently decided. Thus, the suit for partition as filed, could not be said to be barred by Order II Rule 2 of Code, 1908. Plaintiffs could not have claimed interest in the land in the life-time of the decease and the cause of action in the previous suit for declaration of title filed by the decease was materially different. [14]

(iv) It could not be said that the second suit for partition was in respect of the same cause of action as that on which the previous suit was based. In respect of the cause of action of the previous suit Plaintiff was not entitled to more than one relief. Hence, it could not be said that the Plaintiff omitted to sue for relief for which second suit had been filed. Suit for partition with respect to joint property was based on continuing cause of action, as such the suit for partition could not be said to be barred by Order II Rule 2 Code of Civil Procedure. [16]

CHAPTER TWENTY-ONE

Chatti Konati Rao and Ors. vs. Palle Venkata Subba Rao (07.12.2010 – SC) : MANU/SC/1033/2010

Relative Section:

Code of Civil Procedure, 1908 (CPC) - Section 100

Hon'bleJudges/Coram:

H.S. Bedi and C.K. Prasad

Equivalent Citation: AIR2011SC1480, 2011(1)ALT46(SC), 2011 4 AWC4091SC, (SCSuppl) 2011(1) CHN156, 2011(I)CLR(SC)264, 2011-1-LW783, 2011(2)RCR(Civil)824, 2010(13)SCALE173, (2010) 14SCC316

Case Reference:

Asha Devi v. Dukhi Sao MANU/SC/0019/1974 : AIR 1974 SC 2048 : (1974) 2 SCC 492; T. Anjanappa v. Somalingappa MANU/SC/8429/2006 : (2006) 7 SCC 570; Karnataka Board of Wakf v. Government of India and Ors. MANU/SC/0377/2004 : (2004) 10 SCC 779; S.M. Karim v. Bibi Sakina MANU/SC/0236/1964 : AIR 1964 SC 1254; Parsinni v. Sukhi MANU/SC/0575/1993 : (1993) 4 SCC 375; D.N. Venkatarayappa v. State of Karnataka MANU/SC/0766/1997 : (1997) 7 SCC 567; Mahesh Chand Sharma (Dr.) v. Raj Kumari Sharma MANU/SC/0231/1996 : (1996) 8 SCC 128

NumberofPagesintheOriginalJudgment:6

Case Note :

Property - Adverse possession - Title over the property - Suit filed dismissed by the trial court on the ground that no oral evidence was adduced or no document was filed by the Plaintiff to show that the property was entrusted to Defendant-Aggrieved by the judgment and decree of the trial court Plaintiff preferred appeal before the High Court, which was further dismissed- However, the division bench allowed the Letters Patent Appeal --Present appeal preferred by the Heirs and legal representatives of Defendant No-1 - Held, the well settled principle explains that 'Animus possidendi is well known a requisite ingredient of adverse possession. The person who claims adverse possession is required to establish the date on which he came in possession, nature of possession, the factum of possession, knowledge to the true owner, duration of possession and possession was open and undisturbed. The Plaintiff is bound to prove his title as also possession within 12 years and once the Plaintiff proves his title, the burden shifts on the Defendant to establish that he has perfected his title by adverse possession. In the instant case, Appellants failed to prove that they perfected their title by adverse possession. The initial plea of the Appellant was that they had purchased the property from the original owner and alternatively by virtue of agreement to sale they came in possession of the property. The Appellants could not prove the necessary ingredients to establish their title by adverse possession and therefore it was held that the Division Bench was absolutely right in rejecting the Appellants' plea of adverse possession and decreeing the Plaintiff's suit. Hence the judgment and decree of the trial and the appellate Court was set aside-Appeal dismissed.

Facts:

1. Plaintiff No. 1 is the son of Plaintiff No. 2, whereas original Defendant Nos. 1 and 2 were brother and sister of the second Plaintiff. Both the Defendants died during the pendency of the suit. The heirs and legal representatives of the first Defendant were substituted in his place and they had contested the suit.

2. Plaintiff filed the suit for recovery of possession in respect of several properties mentioned in schedule of the plaint and in the present appeal we are concerned with Schedule - I property i.e. four acres of land pertaining to R.S. No. 44/3 situate at village Vijjeswaram, hereinafter referred to as the land in dispute.

3. According to the Plaintiffs their predecessor-in-interest viz., one Venkata Ramana Rao, who happened to be the father of Plaintiff No. 1 and husband of Plaintiff No. 2, was the owner of land in dispute. Venkata Ramana Rao was a Government employee and in his absence Defendant

No. 1 i.e. elder brother of second Plaintiff used to look after his property. Said Venkata Ramana Rao died in the year 1948 and thereafter the Plaintiffs came back to the village and started looking after the agricultural land including the land in dispute. Plaintiff's case further is that again in the year 1954 they shifted their residence to Kakinada for education of the first Plaintiff and Defendant No. 1 was asked to look after the land in dispute. In the year 1974 when the Defendant declined to deliver possession of the land in dispute, lawyer's notice dated 6th April, 1974 was issued calling upon the Defendants to hand over the property. Defendant No. 1 responded to the notice by his letter dated 27th May, 1974 denying the title of the Plaintiffs and claiming himself to be the owner of the property. Plaintiffs thereafter filed the suit bearing O.S. No. 20 of 1974 in the Court of the Subordinate Judge, West Godavari District, Kovvur for recovery of possession in respect of land in dispute and for mesne profit.

4. In the written statement filed by Defendant No. 1 his plea was that he purchased the land in dispute under a stamped agreement from Venkata Ramana Rao for a value of Rs. 1600/-. According to him he paid Rs. 1,000/- to Venkata Ramana Rao and a sum of Rs. 225/- to one Bombothu Chitteyya who was the tenant and in possession of the land in dispute during 1943 and said tenant vide letter dated 16th June, 1943 relinquished his possession and delivered the land to Defendant No. 1. It is further case of Defendant No. 1 that balance amount of Rs. 400/- was sent by Money Order. After the death of Venkata Ramana Rao, the second Plaintiff claimed more money towards the sale of the land in dispute and Plaintiff No. 2 being the sister of Defendant No. 1, a further sum of Rs. 500/- was paid to her vide receipt dated 14th January, 1952 (Exh.B-4).

5. Plea of Defendant No. 1 further is that on 6th November, 1960 he filed an application before the Assistant Settlement Officer for correction of rough patta issued in favour of second Plaintiff in 1959 and to substitute his name along with his brother's name in place of second Plaintiff. In the application Defendant No. 1 categorically stated that on 18th February, 1954 the Settlement Officer directed issuance of patta of the land in dispute along with other lands in their favour and he was all through waiting for the issuance of patta. However, according to Defendant No. 1, in August, 1959 he came to know that a rough patta was issued to second Plaintiff contrary to the decision of the Settlement Officer and thereafter he filed an application on 7th November, 1959 before the Rough Patta Correction Officer informing him about variance between grant and the order and

prayed that the name of the second Plaintiff be deleted from the patta and in her place his name and that of his brother's name be substituted. According to Defendant No. 1 he filed reminder on 6th November, 1960 but it was returned by the Assistant Settlement Officer on 22nd November, 1960 with certain objections. Thereafter the first Defendant did not present the petition for substituting his name in the patta by deleting the name of the second Plaintiff. Further plea of the first Defendant was that he had perfected his title by adverse possession.

Held by Hon'ble Supreme Court

1. In view of the several authorities of this Court, few whereof have been referred above, what can safely be said that mere possession however long does not necessarily mean that it is adverse to the true owner. It means hostile possession which is expressly or impliedly in denial of the title of the true owner and in order to constitute adverse possession the possession must be adequate in continuity, in publicity and in extent so as to show that it is adverse to the true owner. The possession must be open and hostile enough so that it is known by the parties interested in the property. The Plaintiff is bound to prove his title as also possession within 12 years and once the Plaintiff proves his title, the burden shifts on the Defendant to establish that he has perfected his title by adverse possession. Claim by adverse possession has two basic elements i.e. the possession of the Defendant should be adverse to the Plaintiff and the Defendant must continue to remain in possession for a period of 12 years thereafter. Animus possidendi as is well known a requisite ingredient of adverse possession. Mere possession does not ripen into possessory title until possessor holds property adverse to the title of the true owner for the said purpose. The person who claims adverse possession is required to establish the date on which he came in possession, nature of possession, the factum of possession, knowledge to the true owner, duration of possession and possession was open and undisturbed. A person pleading adverse possession has no equities in his favour as he is trying to defeat the rights of the true owner and, hence, it is for him to clearly plead and establish all facts necessary to establish adverse possession. The courts always take unkind view towards statutes of limitation overriding property rights. Plea of adverse possession is not a pure question of law but a blended one of fact and law.

2. Bearing in mind the principles aforesaid when we proceed to consider the facts of this case, we find that Appellants have miserably failed to

prove that they have perfected their title by adverse possession. It is worth mentioning here that initial plea of the Appellant was that they had purchased the property from the original owner, alternatively by virtue of agreement to sale they came in possession of the property. Both these pleas have not been substantiated. Neither the purported sale deed nor agreement to sale have been placed on record. As regards the plea of adverse possession, Appellants' case is that out of the consideration money of Rs. 1,600/-, Rs. 1,000/- was paid to the real owner and on payment of Rs. 225/- to the tenant in possession namely Bombothu Chitteyya, he relinquished his possession. This relinquishment of possession by the tenant shall not enure to the benefit of the Appellants against the true owner so as to accept their claim for adverse possession. Appellants are required to prove that their possession was adverse to the true owner. The plea of the Appellants on the basis of the purported order dated 18th February, 1954 of the Settlement Officer directing for issuance of Patta in their favour also does not advance their case. It is not the Appellant's case that Plaintiffs were party before the Settlement Officer. Further, it is not in dispute that no Patta was issued in favour of the Appellants and in fact rough Patta was issued in favour of the second Plaintiff. Thus, the Appellants have not proved the necessary ingredients to establish their title by adverse possession. In our opinion, the Division Bench is absolutely right in rejecting the Appellants' plea of adverse possession and decreeing the Plaintiff's suit, after setting aside the judgment and decree of the trial and the appellate Court.

3. In the result, we do not find any merit in the appeal and it is dismissed with cost throughout to be paid by the Appellants to the Respondent. Lawyers fee quantified at Rs. 25,000/-.

Adv. Jayprakash Somani's Videos On Law

1) SLP in Supreme Court / Special Leave Petitions in the Supreme Court of India

2) Transfer of Civil & Criminal Cases by the Supreme Court of India / Transfer of Matrimonial Cases

3) Appellate Jurisdiction of the Supreme Court of India

4) Jurisdictions of the Supreme Court of India

5) Public Interest Litigation in the Supreme Court of India / PIL in Supreme Court

6) Article 32 Writ Petitions in the Supreme Court of India

7) Bail Matters Top 10 Supreme Court Cases

8) FIR Quashing in High Court & Supreme Court

9) Bail & Anticipatory Bail Matters in Supreme Court

10) Insolvency & Bankruptcy Matters in the Supreme Court

11) Insolvency & Bankruptcy Code 2016 Part 1

12) Insolvency & Bankruptcy Code 2016 Part 2

13) Insolvency & Bankruptcy Code 2016 Part 3

14) Corporate Liquidation Process

15) Supreme Court Rules & Procedures Webinar of 2.5 hour on Zoom

16) RDDBFI Act, 1993 (Introduction)

17) The Indian Contact Act 1872

18) Negotiable Instruments Act (Introduction)

19) How to avoid matrimonial disputes& some more videos

20) SEBI Matters in the Supreme Court

21) Matrimonial Matters: Supreme Court's 20 Case Laws

22) Consumer Matters Supreme Court's 20 Case Laws

23) Service Matters Supreme Court's 20 Case Laws

24) How to Search Lawyer for Your Matter

25) Property Matters Supreme Court's 20 Case Laws

26) Bail Matters: Supreme Court's 20 Case Laws

27) Supreme Court / High Court Vacation Benches

28) 69000 Teacher's Recruitment Matters of UP Government in the Supreme Court

29) Contempt of Court Matters in the Supreme Court

30) Advocate Act's Matters in the Supreme Court

31) Business Law Matters in the Supreme Court

32) Banking Matters in the Supreme Court

33) Labour Law Matters in the Supreme Court

34) Arbitration Matters in the Supreme Court

35) Careers in Law -Zoom Webinar by Adv. Jayprakash Somani

36) Civil Matters in the Supreme Court

37) Consumer Protection Act | Consumer Matters in the Supreme Court

38) Corporate Matters in the Supreme Court

39) Criminal Matters in the Supreme Court

40) Role of Respondent in the Supreme Court of India

41) Motor Vehicle Accident Matters in Supreme Court with case laws

42) Article 131 Original Suits in Supreme Court

43) PIL in Supreme Court/ Public Interest Litigations in the Supreme Court of India'

44) CAB Citizenship Amendment Bill is not Unconstitutional

45) Supreme Court of India Cases & Process – Marathi

46) Legal Services Export / Export of Legal Services

47) Transfer of Matrimonial Cases by the Supreme Court of India

48) Public Interest Litigation PIL

49) The Specific Relief Act (Introduction)

50) Corporate Insolvency Resolution Process CIRP

51) ABMM's Career 5 - Careers in Law

52) Transfer of cases by Supreme Court

53) Writ Petitions in High Court & Supreme Court of India

54) Supreme Court Jurisdictions - Appeals, SLP, Writ Petitions, Transfer, Original, Review, Curative

55) LEGAL INDIA TV Show: Cases Handled in Supreme Court

56) Corporate Liquidation Process

57) Legal Services Export / Export of Legal Services

58) Corporate Laws

59) Election Matters- Supreme Court's 20 Case Laws

60) Companies Act, 2013

62) Competition Act, 2002

63) Banking Matters - Supreme Court's 20 Case Laws

64) Election Matters in the Supreme Court

65) Armed Forces Tribunal Matters in the Supreme Court

66) Compassionate Appointment Service matter

67) Foreign Exchange Management Act FEMA

68) Foreign Trade Policy 2021-26 Proposed

69) Customs Act 1962

70) Narcotic Drugs and Psychotropic Substances Act, 1985 NDPS Act

71) Foreign Trade Development & Regulation Act, 1992

72) How to Search Good Advocate in the Supreme Court of India

73) Sr. Adv Vikas Singh's Interview in Nani Palkhivala Wednesday Law Club

74) Indian Penal Code (I. P. C.)

75) Criminal Procedure Code (Cr. P. C.)

76) Commercial Courts & International Arbitration - by Mr. Jaideep Gupta, Senior Advocate in Nani Palkhivala Wednesday Law Club

77) Sr. Adv Ranji Thomos in Nani Palkhivala Wednesday Law Club

78) Urgent Matters in Supreme Court during vacations

79) 498A Bail Matters in Supreme Court

81) 376 Bail Matters in Supreme Court

82) 302, 304, 307, 308 Bail Matters in Supreme Court

83) 138, 420 Bail Matters in Supreme Court

84) POCSO Act Bail Matters in Supreme Court

85) NDPS Act Bail Matters in Supreme Court

86) What is ED (Enforcement Directorate)?

87) Prevention of Money Laundering Act, 2002 (PMLA Act)

88) Insolvency & Bankruptcy Code- Supreme Court Case Laws. Webinar in Nani Palkhivala Wednesday Law Club

89) What is NCLT & NCLAT?

90) Acquittal from 376- Supreme Court's some case laws in Nani Palkhivala Wednesday Law Club dt 28.7.22

91) Insolvency & Bankruptcy in India

92) Can we file case directly in the Supreme Court?

93) Adv. Anuja Pethia has cleared AOR Exam 2021 with 77% marks - Her interview in Nani Palkhivala Wednesday Law Club

94) Customs Act - Supreme Court Case Laws & Interview of AOR Adv. Anuja Pethia in Nani Palkhivala Law Club.

95) The Uttar Pradesh Public Service Tribunals Act, 1976

96) POCSO Act - Supreme Court Case Laws & Interview of AOR Adv. Shoumendu Mukharji & Adv. Nishant Verma in Nani Palkhivala Law Club.

97) Who Can Trigger CIRP Process Under Insolvency Law of India

98) The Uttar Pradesh Government Servant Discipline and Appeal Rules, 1999

99) CIRP Application Under Sec 7 by FC

100) Information Technology Act 2000

101) Uttar Pradesh Recruitment of Dependants of Government Servants Dying in Harness Rules, 1974

102) Foreign Exchange Management Act 1999 & Supreme Court's Case Laws on FEMA & Leading Case of AOR Exam in Nani Palkhivala Law Club.

103) Arbitration and Conciliation Act 1996 & It's Supreme Court Case Laws in Nani Palkhivala Wednesday Law Club.

104) Narcotic Drugs & Psychotropic Substances Act 1985 (NDPS Act) & It's Supreme Court Case Laws in Nani Palkhivala Wednesday Law Club.

105) Recovery of Debts and Bankruptcy Act 1993

106) Uttar Pradesh Land Revenue Code 2006

107) CIRP Application Under Sec 9 by OC

108) CIRP Application Under Sec 10 by CD

109) Hindu Succession Act, 1956

110) Maharashtra Civil Services Rules, 1981

111) Indian Contract Act, 1872 & Supreme Court's Case Laws" in Nani Palkhiwala Wednesday Law Club

112) Securities and Exchange Board of India Act, 1992 i. e. SEBI Act 1992 & Case Laws on Insiders Trading" in Nani Palkhiwala Wednesday Law Club

113) Moratorium Under Section 14 of IBC, 2016

114) Hindu Marriage Act, 1955

115) Maharashtra Land Revenue Code, 1966

116) 64 Leading Cases of AOR Exam Session 1 :- Cases 1 to16 in Nani Palkhiwala Wednesday Law Club

117) 64 Leading Cases of AOR Exam Session 2: Cases 17 to 32 in Nani Palkhiwala Wednesday Law Club

118) 64 Leading Cases of AOR Examination Session 3: Cases 33 to 48 in Nani Palkhivala Wednesday Law Club

119) 64 Leading Cases of AOR Exam Session 4: Cases 49 to 64 in Nani Palkhivala Wednesday Law Club

120) Labour Laws of India: Part 1 - 4 New Labour Law Codes of India

121) New Labour Laws Part 2 The Code on Wages, 2019

122) New Labour Laws Part 3:- The Code on Social Security, 2020

123) Argue in English Fluently & Confidently - Two months online course.

124) SLP Admission in the Supreme Court. 2023 (Hindi)

125) Transfer of Petitions from the Supreme Court (Hindi)

126) Review Petition in the Supreme Court.(Hindi)

127) Recovery of debts from the Company (Hindi)

128) How to search 'Good Insolvency & Bankruptcy Consultant?' (HINDI)

129) Curative Petition in the Supreme Court

130) AFT Appeals in the Supreme Court (HINDI)

131) NCLAT's Appeals in the Supreme Court.

132) Transfer Petition: Which matters can we transfer?

133) SLP Types of SLP in the Supreme court of India (English).

134) Argue in English Fluently and Confidently in the High Court & Supreme Court'.

List Of Adv. Jayprakash Somani's Books

1. Supreme Court of India's Leading Case Laws on 'Insolvency & Bankruptcy Code 2016'

2. Bail Matters – Supreme Court's Latest Leading Case Laws

3. Arbitration Matters- Supreme Court's Latest Leading Case Laws

4. Property Matters - Supreme Court's Latest Leading Case Laws

5. Matrimonial Matters- Supreme Court's Latest Leading Case Laws

6. Election Matters- Supreme Court's Latest Leading Case Laws

7.SEBI Matters- Supreme Court's Latest Leading Case Laws

8. Banking Matters- Supreme Court's Latest Leading Case Laws

9. Service Matters- Supreme Court's Latest Leading Case Laws

10. Contempt of Court Matters- Supreme Court's Latest Leading Case Laws

11. Consumer Protection Matters- Supreme Court's Latest Leading Case Laws

12. Corporate Law- Supreme Court's Latest Leading Case Laws

13. Supreme Court's AOR Exam- Leading Cases

14. Armed Force Tribunal - Supreme Court's Latest Leading Case Laws

15. Acquittal From 376 - Supreme Court's Latest Leading Case Laws

16. Negotiable instrument – Supreme Court's Latest Leading Case Laws

17. Contract Act- Supreme Court's Latest Leading Case Laws

18. Insider trading- Supreme Court's Latest Leading Case Laws

19. Foreign Exchange and Management Act- Supreme Court's Latest Leading Case Laws

20. Income Tax Act- Supreme Court's Latest Leading Case Laws

21. Company Law- Supreme Court's Latest Leading Case Laws

22. Competition & Monopoly Matters- Supreme Court's Latest Leading Case Laws

23. Compassionate Appointment- Service Matters- Supreme Court's Latest Leading Case Laws

24. Compulsory Retirement- Service Matters- Supreme Court's Latest Leading Case Laws

25. Voluntary Retirement- Service Matters- Supreme Court's Latest Leading Case Laws

26. Removal/Dismissal/Termination from Service- Supreme Court's Latest Leading Case Laws

27. Seniority- Service Matter- Supreme Court's Latest Leading Case Laws

28. Promotion- Service Matter- Supreme Court's Latest Leading Case Laws

29. Equal Pay for Equal Work- Service Matter- Supreme Court's Latest Leading Case Laws

30. Condition of Service- Service Matter- Supreme Court's Latest Leading Case Laws

31. Customs Act- Supreme Court's Leading Case Laws

32. Information Technology Act- Supreme Court's Leading Case Laws

33. SEC. 125 CR. P. C.- Supreme Court's Leading Case Laws

34. SEC. 498A OF I. P. C.- Supreme Court's Leading Case Laws

35. MOTOR VEHICLE ACT- Supreme Court's Leading Case Laws

36. CONDITION OF SERVICE- SERVICE MATTER- Supreme Court's Leading Case Laws

37. SUSPENSION- SERVICE MATTER- Supreme Court's Leading Case Laws

38. Reservation in SC, ST, OBC- Service Matter- Supreme Court's Leading Case Laws

39. NARCOTIC DRUGS AND PSYCHOTROPIC SUBSTANCES (NDPS) ACT - Supreme Court of India's Latest Leading Case Laws

40. SEC 302 IPC - Supreme Court of India's Latest Leading Case Laws

41. PROTECTION OF CHILDREN FROM SEXUAL OFFENCES ACT (POCSO) - Supreme Court of India's Latest Leading Case Laws

42. PMLA ACT BAIL MATTERS - Supreme Court of India's Leading Case Laws

43. SEC 376 BAIL MATTERS - Supreme Court of India's Leading Case Laws

44. SEC 302 BAIL MATTERS - Supreme Court of India's Leading Case Laws

45. POCSO ACT BAIL MATTERS - Supreme Court of India's Leading Case Laws

46. JUVENILE JUSTICE ACT- Supreme Court of India's Leading Case Laws

47. TRANSFER OF PROPERTY ACT- Supreme Court of India's Leading Case Laws

48. PROFESSIONAL ETHICS OF ADVOCATES- AOR EXAM- SUPREME COURT'S LEADING CASE LAWS

49. TRANSFER OF PROPERTY ACT- Supreme Court of India's Leading Case Laws

50. WHITE COLLAR CRIME- SUPREME COURT'S LEADING CASE LAWS

51. SEC 302 BAIL MATTERS- SUPREME COURT'S LEADING CASE LAWS

Books are available online in India

1. Notion Press: https://notionpress.com/author/jayprakash_somani

2. Amazon: https://www.amazon.in/s?k=jayprakash+somani

3. Flipkart: https://www.flipkart.com/search?q=Jayprakash%20Somani

Books are available online at International Market

4. Amazon International: https://www.amazon.com/s?k=jayprakash+somani

5. Amazon United Kingdom: https://www.amazon.co.uk/s?k=jayprakash+somani

6. E-Books/Kindle edition at National & International Level: https://www.amazon.in/s?k=jaypraksh+somani